Burnt I. Harbor

Thorofare

R

arter Creek

Old Cove

Airy Ledge

th
tone
ge

Green Ledge

COOMBS MTN.

ut

HAUT

Richs Cove

Dolliver Island

York Ledges

BAY

MT. CHAMPLAIN

Rabbits Ear

York Island

SAWYER MTN.

ERUSALEM MTN.

The Turnip Yard

The Cow Pen

Great Meadow

Battery

POND

Horseman Pt

Little Spoon Island

L. TRAIL Pond Pond

Long

Seal Ledges

Boom Beach

White Horse

Sheep Thief

Black Horse

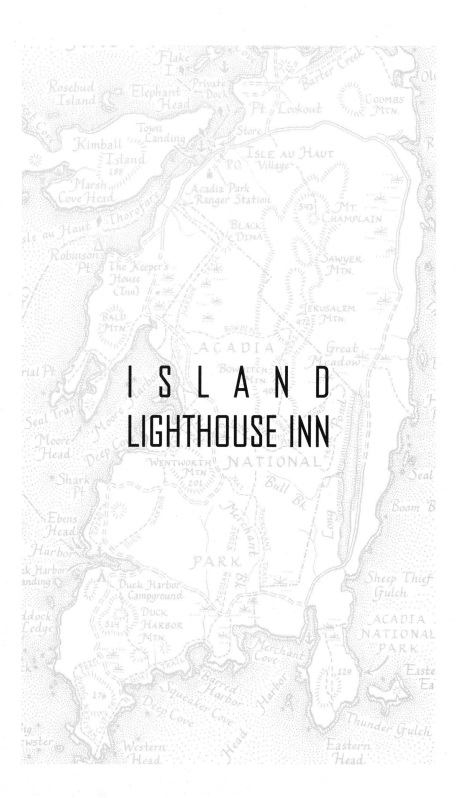

ISLAND
LIGHTHOUSE INN

ISLAND LIGHTHOUSE INN

A CHRONICLE

JEFFREY BURKE

The Pilgrim Press
Cleveland, Ohio

The Pilgrim Press, Cleveland, Ohio 44115

Printed in the United States of America on acid-free paper

02 01 00 99 98 97   5 4 3 2 1

Library of Congress Cataloging-in-Publication Data
Burke, Jeffrey, 1943–
    Island lighthouse inn : a chronicle / Jeffrey Burke.
      p.   cm.
    ISBN 0-8298-1162-1 (cloth)
    1. Cookery, American—New England style.   2. Bed and
    breakfast accommodations—Maine—Isle au Haut—
    History.   3. Isle au Haut (Me.)—Anecdotes.   4. Keeper's
    House Inn—Maine—Isle au Haut—History.   I. Title.
TX715.2.N48B87   1997   96-37601
647.94741′5303—dc21   CIP

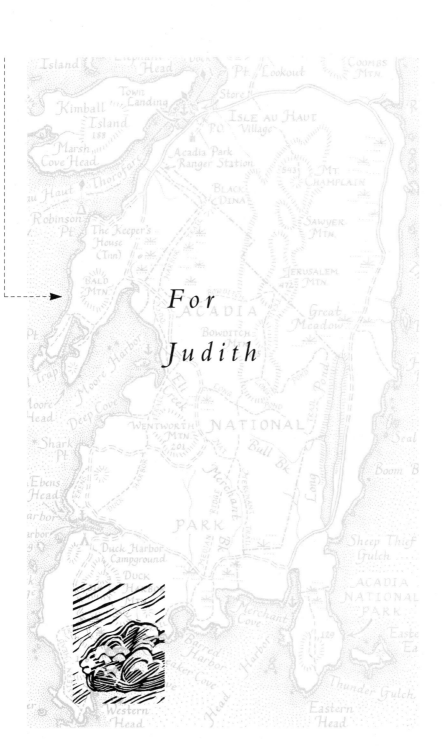

For

Judith

CONTENTS

RECIPES IN THIS BOOK

PREFACE

I NEVER ASKED FOR THIS LIFE—living in a run-down light-house on a rocky island off the coast of Maine, taking in a procession of strange travelers to pay for its renovation. It simply fell in my lap, me, Jeffrey Burke, fugitive social worker/cabinetmaker/community activist, fleeing the numbed suburbs of California with my wife and three kids. We sought a more gratifying life, something New England–like: traditional, peaceful, and quaint. But as usual, things spun out of my control, a hurtling sequence of bizarre events, one after the other, until one frosty October morning we found ourselves cast on this faraway isle.

What follows are my recollections of the odder happenings during our first ten years as fledgling innkeepers here at the lighthouse, stories interwoven with Judi's most popular recipes and bits of our personal odyssey, a smattering of social observations, an occasional tirade of conscience. In the course of these experiences, I have been birthed, kicking and screaming, into the second half of my life, still outraged by injustice, still frustrated by my inability to make the world the way I want it, and still

dazed by the consequences of my silly attempts. But after a
decade on this island, I'm a little wiser, a lot happier.
Hopefully, sharing this saga will offer an occasional insight,
a chuckle or two, and help ease the reader along his or her
own path.

Now, before we get started, let's have a cup of oolong
tea and a slice of Phoebe's Chocolate Birthday Cake . . .

PHOEBE'S CHOCOLATE
BIRTHDAY CAKE

When Phoebe, my friend's daughter, came to the lighthouse to celebrate her third birthday, she requested a
chocolate cake with blueberries and whipped cream. It
became a winner at the Keeper's House and now gets
served with raspberries and strawberries too. Phoebe is
now ten years old and still comes to help me at the inn
and ride Thunder, my horse.

—from *Kitchen with a View,* by Judi Burke

    I cup butter
    I 3/4 cups sugar
    2 eggs
    2 Tbs. vanilla
    2 1/4 cups white flour
    I 1/2 tsp. baking powder
    1/2 tsp. baking soda
    1/2 tsp. salt
    1/2 cup cocoa
    I cup buttermilk
    I cup boiling water

▲ Cream butter and sugar until fluffy. Beat in eggs one at a time. Beat in
vanilla. Sift together flour, baking powder, salt, and cocoa. Stir dry mixture into butter/sugar mixture alternately with buttermilk, beating after
each addition until smooth. Stir in boiling water. Bake 30 to 35 minutes
at 350 degrees, in two greased 9-inch round pans that have been sprin-
kled lightly with cocoa. Frost with chocolate icing or serve with fresh
berries and whipped cream.

CHOCOLATE ICING FOR
PHOEBE'S CAKE

3 squares unsweetened chocolate
3 Tbs. butter
1 1/2 cups confectioner's sugar
1/4 cup hot milk
1 tsp. vanilla

Melt chocolate and butter slowly. Remove from heat. Stir in confectioner's sugar. Slowly add milk to make a spreading consistency. Beat until
smooth. Stir in vanilla.

ACKNOWLEDGMENTS

MY THANKS to Jennifer Hadley, Nancy Hodermarsky, Brenda Gilchrist, Siri Beckman, Tom Batt, Harold and Ruth VanDoren, and Al Gordon for their technical coaching and patience (commas *always* go inside quotations); to Bob DeWitt, Davyne Verstandig, and Peter Frisbie for steadfast rooting; to Carolyn Page and Roy Zarucchi for my first glance at the publishing world; and to Richard Brown and the folks at Pilgrim Press for taking a chance on an unproven author. Judi's recipes are especially welcome.

To the Spirit of Stephanie Levy, my most profound appreciation: her keen pencil and affirming words helped me most of all.

IN MEMORIAM

ROBIN, WHOSE GENEROSITY AND FAITH in the human spirit made the Keeper's House possible, stood on the shore back in Massachusetts several years after we opened. It was mid-March, and a nasty nor'easter was pounding the beach. Maybe he was wondering what the storm had to teach him. Maybe he wanted to understand the soul of the sea. Maybe he wished to intensify his search for the perfect world. Whatever his reasons, he launched his skiff, scrambled in, and pushed off into the breakers. He pulled hard on the oars and the skiff plunged seaward, his arcing strokes as powerful and graceful as the beat of an eagle's wings. Further out he went, this lover of the ocean, this builder of boats crafted to sail with gods, this navigator who knew the routes of clouds through the heavens and fish through the sea. Further he went. With his thin body hunched over the oars and spray erupting over the bow, the transom sunk lower and lower as the seas rose around him. Without a missed stroke, without varying his course a single compass point, he rowed straight into the teeth of that howling gale. Still further he went, further and further and further. Eventually, the wind and sea thrashed so mightily the sky was swept clean of light, the horizon bare of man.

Wunnish, Robin.

xvii

PROLOGUE: FROM CASTRO VALLEY, CALIFORNIA, TO PEMAQUID, MAINE

May 11, 1982

BY THE TIME MY SON PETER AND I had rented the Ryder truck and returned to Carlton Avenue, a dozen friends were gathered in front of our house. They waited in the yard, staring silently at the jumble of cardboard boxes and disassembled furniture. Judi had stopped packing. She sat on the door stoop sipping tea with our friends Rita and Terrie, speaking of journals to be kept, letters to be written. Our youngest, Matthew, seven years junior to Peter, wandered up and down the cluttered driveway clutching a knapsack of comic books and dragging his sleeping bag, waiting for someone to direct him. I supposed Dawn was still lingering in her bedroom where I'd left her earlier, sobbing while she collected her things from the drawers of her bureau: her baby teeth, her school photos, a dried-out rose from her twelfth birthday party. I bounded from the truck cab, eager to organize the loading. What an adventure, moving to Maine!

"O.K.!" I shouted. "Let's get the big things first, the mattresses and power tools and tables and stuff." Nobody moved. Underneath the weeping willow, my friend Joe stood apart from all

the others, hands sunk in pockets, gazing at the ground. Judi
and I had met him in Venezuela in 1966 while we were all
in the Peace Corps organizing marketing cooperatives and
latrine-digging projects. When Judi and I returned to the
States with baby Peter, we spent a dismal summer in New
York City working for the Welfare Department. Frustrated
with the massive bureaucracy and the hopelessness of the
South Bronx, we had moved to California. In the San
Francisco Bay area, we were reunited with Joe and his new
wife, Rita. Together with four other ex-volunteers, we
became immersed in the antiwar movement and the cam-
paign to democratize unions. The eight of us settled com-
munally in a sprawling old house in Oakland, with Peter
and Dawn, then a toddler, and Rita and Joe's new baby,
Ernesto Che. Back then, at the beginning of the '70s, we
believed we could change the world.

Joe shuffled over and kicked the front tire of the
Ryder.

"What about the cold?" he said. "You guys will freeze
in Maine. Your blood is too thin for subzero weather."

"We need you here to organize," insisted Bob. He and
Judi had organized the union at the Hayward Xerox plant.
Behind his wire-rimmed glasses, his eyes burned as brightly
as ever. "If you wanna fight bosses and smash the state,
California's where it's at. We set the trend for the rest of the
nation: don't you want to stay here in the vanguard?"

Rita came over with Judi. "I think you're making a big
mistake," she insisted. "All your friends are here. Your jobs.
And you've got family here. How can you simply pack and
leave? It isn't fair."

"And what about culture?" asked Fred, my U. C.
Berkeley buddy. He slung a crate of dishes onto the tailgate,
his ponytail bobbing. "What can Maine offer you besides
square dances and yodeling contests? And the cuisine? Here

you have your choice from Mexican to Sudanese. You want to trade all that for clam chowder and baked beans?"

The separation from our friends stretched from hour to hour. So hard to say goodbye. We had stood picket duty with them through long nights in front of the gates at General Motors, been thrown in jail together, red-baited, taunted, knocked on our asses at union meetings. We had partied together, too, trekked the High Sierra, picnicked every May Day in Tilden Regional Park and, on hot Sunday afternoons, basked naked on the hidden beaches in Marin. And every evening, we all had lingered around our communal table to feast on fresh produce salvaged from the dumpster behind the local Safeway market, sharing stories about our organizing struggles in the factories where we worked, and dreaming always about how to make the world a better place. For three wonderful years our commune flourished, but as the kids grew older and each of us developed our own individual interests, we no longer were bound by a common goal. The commune dissolved.

Judi and I had spent twenty years trying to change the system. There had been victories, of course, a life redirected here and there, an organizing drive won—and the eventual end of the Vietnam War. But by the late '70s things weren't the same anymore: the robust tribal spirit in the streets of Berkeley and Oakland had drained away. Too much drugs. Too much anarchy. Too little positive change.

Judi and I and the kids (by then we had all three) had eventually moved into the house in Castro Valley, still hoping our lives could make a difference. But our patterns had begun to reflect the larger world: we worked from 7 to 4 five days a week in jobs that became boring and meaningless; we commuted long distances on crowded freeways; we lived in a haze of smog that rarely lifted; we had our house broken into and burgled, Peter's bicycle stolen, Dawn

threatened at school. And the bills! They never stopped
mounting. Worst of all, more than once during dinner the
drinking glasses jiggled and the house began to shake—we
would scramble under the table until the tremors passed.
When would the Big One come?

We had to get ourselves away.

A year before, we had visited my brother Steve and his
family on the coast of Maine, where the grass stays green all
summer long, school grounds are clear of litter, villages
thrive without shopping malls, and strangers wave from
passing cars. Looked pretty good to me. But if we abandoned the factories and inner cities of California, would we
be running away from our duty to purge the world of
problems? Besides, moving to the hinterlands of Maine
seemed a risky chance to take: in California we both had
jobs that paid well, and for the first time ever the kids were
leading comparatively normal lives.

On New Year's Day Judi and I had taken a walk down
by Lake Chabot. Using the back of my pay stub from the
Kenlab Sheetmetal Company, we listed reasons to go, reasons to stay, the consequences of our decisions, the long-
haul payoffs, the potential disasters.

"I've always wanted a horse," said Judi. "Maybe we
would finally have the space . . . and the time to ride. I'd
need a little barn, of course."

Our resolution: by mid-May we'd have the kids'
schoolwork completed for the year and be on our way to
Maine to open a bed-and-breakfast inn.

Now, on this spring day in 1982, it was time to go. We
managed to jam most of our belongings into the Ryder.
Maggie, our Great Dane, bounded into the back of our
Toyota camper with Matthew, Judi slowly climbing behind
the wheel. Dawn sat beside her, still crying as she fastened
her seat belt. Peter swung into the Ryder with me as if he

were mounting the seat of a Conestoga wagon to ride shot-gun across the prairie. Amid the tears and farewells, we pulled away, the last unwanted relics of our old lives scattered across the uncut lawn.

We climbed out of Castro Valley onto Interstate 80. Across the city we convoyed, suspended on the skyway, past the Port of Oakland, past the teeming lanes of traffic curling toward the Bay Bridge, past the Berkeley salt flats, heading for another ocean, three thousand miles away.

IN PEMAQUID, MAINE, WE FOUND an old clapboard farmhouse nestled in the crook of a stream. Below, a broad salt cove spread between the spruce. Great blue herons and ospreys glided in, plucking spawning alewives from the millpond by the house. We bought it on the spot. After a week of feverish work, we opened our bed-and-breakfast, the Little River Inn. Judi went wild in the kitchen, discovering exotic new breakfasts she never had time to make in California: fancy egg soufflés and rich buttermilk biscuits, apple muffins and Finnish pancakes. She also adopted a horse named Thunder.

Peter and Matthew sulked, disappointed that Maine wasn't all I had promised. But on the afternoon of a visit to her new school, Dawn pitched a perfect baseball game, striking out seventeen batters, and fell in love with a kid named Horace.

Over the next three years, I renovated the buildings and groomed the grounds until the inn was perfect. In the evenings, I received guests and helped them plan their itineraries. Often, after a day on the shore and a meal of lobster and clams on Small Brothers Wharf, a guest or two would wander into the parlor to sit with me and chat. We stayed up late, stoking the wood stove, discussing philoso-

phies of life, and sharing dreams about how the world
should be. Friendships were born. That's how I met Robin.
That's how I met Jay. And that's where I first heard about
the derelict lighthouse on Isle au Haut . . . and that's where
this chronicle goes.

OUR FAMOUS FINNISH

PANCAKES

2 eggs
2 cups milk
1 cup sifted flour
2 Tbs. sugar
2 Tbs. butter
fresh fruit
1/2 cup plain yogurt or sour cream

Beat eggs together with milk. Add sifted flour and 1 tablespoon sugar.
Beat until smooth. Put butter in a deep pie or quiche dish and melt in
oven. Pour batter over melted butter and sprinkle with remaining sugar.
Bake 40 minutes at 350 degrees. Top with fresh fruit (strawberries, raspberries, blueberries, or sliced apples sautéed in 2 tablespoons butter, 2
tablespoons maple syrup, a dash of cinnamon, and a dash of nutmeg).
Top with a dollop of yogurt or sour cream. Serves 4. Scrumptious yet simple: a great international treat to bring folks together.

1

SPIRIT STORM

November 30, 1985

AT FIRST LIGHT I WAS JARRED AWAKE by the squeal of a car careening to a stop outside the Little River Inn. In our bedroom in the gable above the driveway, arriving autos usually flood our walls with light, but this maniac had barreled down the winding road without his headlights on: Robin was back.

"Headlights ruin your night vision," he always said. "*That's* what causes accidents—you see only what they illuminate, a narrow tunnel through the world. Think of the nocturnal joys you miss: the breathing woods, the sky above, the creatures all around. Ban the headlight! Cars should prowl the highways like panthers in the night."

Propped on my elbow, I peered out the window. His slim, shadowy silhouette uncoiled from the Volvo and slipped around the corner of the barn. I knew he would be positioning himself at the top of Fawcett's hayfield, facing east (every morning he greeted the day with the "sun salutation," his morning yoga exercise). I fumbled for my jeans, pulled them on, and started downstairs. Shortly, Robin would be banging

around in the kitchen making a cup of herbal tea and
scouring the refrigerator for leftovers.

Every six weeks he made a two-night reservation with
us. Using our B&B as his base of operations, he proffered
his newest brainstorms to local boatbuilders, "spiritually
connected," "earth-friendly" New Age gizmos like electronic sensors to communicate with whales, hulls designed
to carry the soul to the Happy Hunting Grounds, and sails
purified by the incantations of Wampanoag medicine men.
What metaphysical mumbo-jumbo had he brought with
him this time? I tolerated his foolishness because he always
paid up front and never left a mess. And, the truth is, his
crazy ideas about how the world should be often appealed
to me, although Judi thought he was nuts. At times, though,
he really pissed me off—like now, arriving at the crack of
dawn and waking all our guests, knowing we wouldn't have
his room ready until well after ten.

I made my way down to the kitchen, remembering
how I first met Robin: he fell through our gallery ceiling.
Judi had checked him in. After he had unpacked his things,
he wandered up to the attic with his harmonicas to blow
blues where the acoustics were good. In an unfloored storage area, he had stepped between the floor joists and broken through the plaster. Amid the splintered lath and falling
dust his lanky legs dangled, the rubble raining into a bin of
photographs. Damn, was I mad! He had insisted on buying
plasterboard and paint and helping me with the repairs. In
the process, a vacillating friendship was born, contingent on
my level of tolerance for his wacky behavior.

He loved helping out at the inn. He would run around
the front lawn with the mower, always leaving jagged fur-
rows of uncut grass ("refuges for valuable insects," he said),
and he would insist on washing dishes after every meal,
although he refused to use soap or hot water (that was

"wasting resources," or "supporting atomic power," or "introducing nonsoluble toxins into the water table").

When he'd completed his round to the local boatyards, Robin packed his papers and thingumajigs back into the Volvo and left me with a firm *abrazo,* a warm smile, and his Wampanoag salute.

"*Wunnish* (Be well)," he would say.

Over the course of several years, I learned a lot about Robin. He had once been a successful businessman: big house down in Massachusetts, cute wife and smart kids, lots of flashy cars, yachts, disposable income, the works. But material wealth had never made him happy, and his frustration with the values of the business world had led him to smoke lots of pot, an escalating habit that carried his mind into a different dimension. He drifted toward the Native American peoples and adopted their languages, beliefs, and medicine, their understanding of harmony between nature and spirit. His suits and ties disappeared. He became a sort of left-wing Johnny Appleseed, wandering throughout New England, supporting any cause that aids the human spirit. He became convinced that he could communicate with coyotes and clouds and the fish in the sea, bugs and birds and lumps of granite. Every animal, flower, and insect has a lesson to teach us, he said, if we only make the effort to listen. For instance, while we were out for a walk down by Oslin's Cove, he fell to his knees in the mud flats, scooped up a handful of muck, and devoured it on the spot, in order to experience the life of a clam.

"Caw, caw, caw."

The familiar voice from the wild came from outside the inn's back entrance, but I knew it wasn't a crow: the mudroom door swung open and Robin walked in, ducking slightly so his willowy frame could clear the low doorway. Dignified, with short graying hair, to the casual observer he

looked like an insurance salesman—but the leather and
feathers always gave him away. His belts were hand-tooled
by friends from the Oglala nation, and the deerskin pouch
he always carried was laced with beads and tipped with bits
of raven feathers. In it, he carried his cures and the potent
herb which kept his eyes aglow.

Robin bowed like a samurai. Then he covered the
kitchen with a single stride and gave me a bear hug.
"*Wunnish*. May you be well," he said.

"Hi, Robin," I answered.

I always greeted him with ambivalent affection. At
times I enjoyed him enormously, but somehow he always
screwed things up. His flaky sense of priorities, his insis-
tence on being correct, his moral outrage when he saw
injustice: there was always something that made him cause
a scene. Invariably, though, each time he visited his warmth
and humanity brought us closer together.

And on this particular occasion, I was waiting for him
anxiously: I had a need to talk with him.

He looked me over, sensing I was not myself.

I put on the teakettle. He helped himself to a huge
bowl of Judi's homemade granola. He sat down, his spidery
legs akimbo, his pointy knees canting out to clear the
kitchen table.

"What's going on?" he asked. "Are the spirits not with
you?"

"I've had a great disappointment, Robin. Last month I
discovered a most remarkable place, a distant island named
Isle au Haut. While I was there, a great opportunity passed
me by."

He looked straight at me and read the loss in my eyes.
He pulled his Buck knife from his pocket and sliced bananas
onto his granola, then flooded the bowl with lukewarm
water. His spoon shoveled away at the mountain of cereal.

"Tell me what happened," he said.

I poured us each a cup of tea and joined him at the table. "It all happened so fast, Robin: Judi and I got an invitation to meet a friend up the coast and . . ."

This is what I told him.

The Captain's Quarters Motel
Stonington, Maine
October 17, 1985
6:00 A.M.

Judi and I crawled from our blankets. We had an hour to get dressed, have a cup of coffee, and get down to the landing to board *Mink,* the mailboat to Isle au Haut. Brisk air seeped in around the windows, warning us to dress warmly for the six-mile passage down Penobscot Bay. Muffled stirrings came from adjacent rooms: the other members of our expedition were getting ready, too (they had all checked in the night before and gone to bed before we arrived). One by one, we greeted each other as we stumbled into the public area of the motel, an assemblage of old wood frame buildings knitted together with passageways and decks hanging over Stonington Harbor.

The two members of the Lighthouse Preservation Society who organized our trip were already waiting: Jay Hyland, founder and chairman of the society, and Valerie Nelson, the society's executive director. We had met Jay a year before while he was doing a survey on the deteriorating condition of New England lighthouses. Caught in a summer storm, he had sought refuge at the Little River Inn, appearing at our door sopping wet with a sheaf of photographs under his arm.

Then, several days ago, we had gotten a call from Jay, asking us to rendezvous in Stonington for a mysterious early-morning trip to Isle au Haut.

"Keep the lights shining, Jeff," Jay said as he strode across the lobby to shake my hand. He is a bookish-looking fellow, pleasant and well mannered, with a neatly trimmed mustache and carefully pressed shirt and slacks, unusual attire along the coast of Maine. He always totes reams of documents, proposals, and photographs.

"We've got to find a way to save the Isle au Haut lighthouse station," he said. "She's been boarded up for years—paint is scabbing off the keeper's house, windows are cracked, roof is ready to go. Now it's for sale."

"Sounds desirable enough to me," I said. "How come no one has snatched it up?"

Valerie set her teacup down on the coffee table.

"Too remote," she said, rising to join us at the picture window looking across the harbor. "With no telephone or power, no dock to land a boat, no ferry to deliver cars, the moneyed benefactors we usually recruit for sponsors find the hardships too repelling. But we've got to act fast—the elements are devastating to unprotected towers."

While Jay was the technical wizard for the society, Valerie seemed to be the spokesperson.

"Our board of directors is excited about this one, Jeff," said Jay. "It could be a precedent for saving these off-shore lights. On the mainland there is usually support to retrofit them into museums, restaurants, even youth hostels. But way out here in the middle of the ocean . . ." Jay shrugged his shoulders and smiled quizzically. "We've asked you to come along while we investigate, to see if you and Judi think this one is suitable for vacationers of a more adventurous type."

Last to emerge from his room was Aubrey Greenlaw, the owner of the lighthouse station. A robust man with a broad smile and straight-combed hair, he circled the motel lobby pouring coffee and handing out doughnuts. The station had been in his family since 1935, when his grandfather bought it at a government auction. After using the place intermittently for fifty years, three generations of Aubrey's family had tired of the responsibility and the cost of maintenance. It was his task to find a new owner.

We finished our coffee and bustled outside. Brightly painted lobster boats lay motionless across the harbor, glued to the surface of the water, their bows pointing in unison toward the coming tide. Boat houses and bait shacks built on long-legged piers crowded the shore, their decks cluttered with lobster traps and mounds of herring seine.

Aubrey led the way to the mailboat landing: there waited *Mink,* a bullish forty-six-foot Jarvis-Newman with an enclosed and heated cabin, built in Southwest Harbor, 44,000 pounds of timber, fiberglass, and brass, powered by a 4104 380-horsepower Caterpillar, mean enough to bore through any seas Penobscot Bay could offer. Her engine idled heavily, her green cabin top glistening with frost. On deck, a stocky, bull-necked young mate scratched away the icy dust with a luminescent broom.

"Watch yer step," he called up to us with a genuine smile. "It's wicked slick down here."

Cautiously, we descended the ramp to *Mink,* then clambered through the cabin door to be greeted by a gust of warm air and the odor of diesel fuel.

The captain turned and faced us. His name was Buster. From behind his thick eyeglasses, he surveyed

our out-of-town crew, evaluating the way we were
dressed, the texture of our skin. He wore a baseball cap
with a Caterpillar logo and generic green work clothes,
his trousers held up with a pair of red striped sus-
penders. Clenched in his teeth was a smoldering pipe.
He glared at us and spoke.

"Who's in charge of yer outfit?" he demanded.

Aubrey had the courage to speak. (He had known
Buster for years, even though Buster hardly nodded to
him when we boarded the boat.)

"We're here with the Lighthouse Preservation
Society, Buster, to take a look at the station on Robinson
Point. There may be a possibility these folks could find a
way to turn the old place into a bed-and-breakfast inn."

Buster grinned like the Cheshire cat.

"Well," he chuckled, wagging his head in disbelief,
"I've heard of some foolish proposals for that ragtag
place, but that's got to be the goddamn silliest one yet."

He sucked on the pipe, checked his watch, gave a
warning blast on the foghorn, and turned to the wheel.
Tim, the mate, glided through the cabin and let off the
stern line. *Mink* eased away from the dock. Over his
shoulder, Buster closed our conversation.

"I come back at noon sharp, so be at the landing by
then or you'll be sleeping in the woods."

We set off down the bay. Pressed against the cabin
windows, we watched Stonington recede behind a
string of spruce-clad islands. For an hour, Buster wove
Mink between the granite outcroppings, often veering
sharply to avoid ledges lurking beneath the surface.
Then we swung toward the highest island and entered
the Thorofare, the passageway that gives shelter to the
village of Isle au Haut. Expertly, Buster brought *Mink*
into the landing and got us all ashore.

Two fenderless pickups sputtered down to the dock to pick up supplies arriving on the boat. While Tim unloaded freight, Buster ambled up to the road, lifted the hood on an ancient Chrysler station wagon, and twisted its battery cables into place. After several failed attempts, he finally got it smoking and jerked down the road to the post office to pick up the mail.

Aubrey led us the opposite way, down a one-lane patch of tar that trailed along the shore before fading into a path. We hurried along, chattering about the possibility of an island lighthouse inn. Soon, the dense spruce closed in on us and the magic of the forest began to demand our attention. We walked in silence, strung out along the path, entranced by the fiery autumn blueberry bushes, the momentary dash of an eight-point buck, the ever-present sea surrounding us, never more that a ribbon of forest away.

Woods gave way to shore again. Our path climbed sharply along the cliffs. On one side the ocean surged among the rocks below; on the other, the forest leaned against us, pushing us toward the sea. Carcasses of giant blown-down trees lay rotting in the mossy darkness.

Finally, we pushed through a stand of saplings and found a collapsed and crumbling gate: it was the boundary line of the lighthouse station. The pale blue gables of the keeper's house rose above the green, and as we broke into the open the granite and brick light tower jutted into the sky. On three sides we were surrounded by water.

"What a beauty!" Jay exclaimed. "She was built in 1907, the last one erected in Maine. She's a doozy, too; they had money back then to do things right: fancy keeper's house with original moldings, storage sheds, oil house, and a nifty boat barn built right on the shore. What an opportunity!"

"How does the light work if there is no power, no one to keep it running?" I asked, craning my neck to study the lantern room.

"See that blue panel mounted to the catwalk?" Jay said, gesturing up through the spruce boughs. "That's a photovoltaic panel. It uses sunlight to charge the batteries protected inside the tower; they power the beacon. The beam stands forty-eight feet above mean high tide, with a red warning sector aimed across the bay to ward ships away from subsurface ledges."

Jay recited a hundred facts about the light. He knew everything about it, and the brightness in his eyes intensified with each statistic. No longer was he an office-bound administrator; his presence here made him come alive.

We circled the boarded-up house admiring the high white stucco walls and the immense blocks of cut granite that formed its foundation. Middling conifers and thick bayberry encroached on the once well-tended grounds, and tufts of grass filled the spaces between the slabs of the walkways. In shady places, moss had grown across the concrete: there had been no passing boots to keep it worn away.

Aubrey jiggled an iron key in the back door. It squeaked open. We filed in. A cast-iron cookstove filled one side of the kitchen. By the sink, a hand pump had been mounted, ready to draw water from the cellar cistern. Behind the pantry doors were stacks of old dishes with cobalt blue swirls around their edges, and nests of dented pots blackened by years of use. An empty flour barrel stowed beneath the counter seemed to be waiting to be refilled. Everything appeared frozen in time, as if the light keeper's family might return, sailing back up the Thorofare with provisions from the mainland.

Each room was a new discovery. Old furniture
crowded against the walls. Relics filled the closets: crib-
bage boards, worn clothes, old photographs. Gaslights
had decent mantles and sufficient fuel, ready to illuminate the pastel paint. Threadbare spreads were pulled
evenly over beds. Chimney brushes and kerosene cans
were neatly stored on the cellar landing. In spite of the
cracked plaster, the musty smells, and the overgrown
grounds, the lighthouse station had been reverently protected; not a thing had changed in fifty years.

For two hours we explored. We crawled through a
trap door into the attic and descended the basement
stairs. We plowed through the junk in the woodshed
and climbed up into the rafters of the boathouse. We
scouted the surrounding woods, inspected the outhouse,
poked at the sills, and checked the shingles. We peeked
into old trunks, flopped on the mattresses, rocked in the
chairs. We walked the boundaries, climbed the hill, scuttled along the shore. We envisioned. We fantasized. We
dreamed.

Over the years the weather had gotten to the
buildings, but they were basically sound. The station
needed far more than paint and plaster, however: no
road wound its way to the lighthouse door, and the
landing ways on the shore had rotted out decades ago.
There had never been a water well; hence, no plumbing, no bathrooms, no sewage system. The island had no
telephones, and the closest power line was a mile away
in the village.

I loved it! It was like the finest stretched canvas,
with the basic forms sketched in, ready for the creation
of a masterpiece.

Aubrey grew subdued, perhaps sensing our
enchantment and realizing his family ties to their old

homestead might soon be severed. Jay and Valerie could
see the gleam in my eyes, too. They knew the creation
of an island lighthouse inn would be a landmark victory
for lighthouse preservation. They suggested Judi and I
buy it.

"You're the perfect people to do it," said Jay, his
mustache whisking with excitement.

Valerie chimed in, "We'll dress you in little sailor
suits and you can give your guests slide shows on
Victorian lighthouse architecture, turn the station into a
museum, and start a stampede of enthusiasm to save the
nation's lights!"

My head was reeling with different images: I envisioned a living form of art, where visitors become an
active element in a collage of natural beauty, classic
buildings, wholesome food, and the music of woods and
sea, all stirred alive by the phallic majesty of the pulsing
lighthouse.

Judi didn't like it.

"No," she said.

"But Judi, I can feel it in my bones . . ."

"No," she said again.

I said, "We can't let this opportunity slip by. It's a
phenomenon waiting to happen. Think of the attraction
these historic buildings have! It's a vacationer's dream,
can't you see? People would come from across the
country to escape the madness of the cities, to . . ."

"No," she said, once more.

"But Judi, you don't understand. Why, the mailboat
alone is a fantastic attraction. And people are bored with
snooty hotels. They'd stand in line to come, to experience
something more than the dreary familiarity of electric
lights and telephones and private baths, room service and
valet parking, saunas and faxes and beauty salons . . ."

"No," she said, one more time.

I said, "It would be an immediate success. And think of what a wonderful life we'd have: no traffic or hassles or pollution or crime."

She said, "Jeffrey, we just made new friends back in Pemaquid . . . and I finally have my horse after waiting for so many years. And anyway, I'm afraid of the ocean. And I like cooking only breakfast for guests—here they'd need lunch and dinner, too! I can't handle that. And realistically, Jeffrey, think of all the expense—it would take a fortune to restore this shabby place. We don't have a penny."

I said, "But Judi, this isn't just any ordinary old place . . ."

But I was losing ground. The more I argued, the less sense it made. And Judi wasn't the only naysayer; it was a scheme the banks would never touch. We had no assets to cash in, no strings to pull. Back in Pemaquid, our three needy children waited, along with a drawer of unpaid bills, our neurotic Great Dane Maggie, and Judi's forever-hungry horse. The creation of this lighthouse inn was beyond my reach. Who would Jay ask instead?

I could have sulked forever, but it was getting late. Buster would be ready to cast off, and we all had a long drive ahead once we got back to the mainland. For me, it would be a sobering ride.

We gathered up our belongings and were about to start back to the boat landing when, suddenly, the wind began to howl and whitecaps appeared where only moments before the water rolled in gentle swells. Below where we stood, waves crashed in, sending sheets of spray in the sky, carried by a mounting wind that whipped my jacket collar. We turned and hurried toward the boat landing, worried that the bay might be too rough to

cross. In spite of my disappointment about the lighthouse, I was fascinated by that change in the weather.

ROBIN LISTENED TO ME FINISH MY STORY. Then he pushed
aside his empty cereal bowl, got to his feet, walked to the
kitchen window, and gazed at Oslin's Cove down across the
hayfield.

"Spirit storm," he said.

"What?" I said.

"Spirit storm," he repeated. "That change in the sea
you witnessed—it was a spirit storm. It's good stuff, man—
an auspicious sign of powerful forces, of great changes in
the making."

Lots of times Robin made no sense at all. I expected a
little advice, though, but Robin turned and left, tramping
across the lawn and scaling the tallest pine by the library
path (whenever he had something on his mind, he would
shinny up a tree, hang upside-down like a possum, and med-
itate). I expected him back in time for lunch, but shortly
after, I heard his Volvo squeal out the drive. He never came
back that day and didn't bother to call. If he had only let
me know, at least I could have rented his room to some
other party.

A few days later, an envelope arrived. Inside was a
check and a note:

JEFF . . . THIS SHOULD COVER THE DOWN PAYMENT.
                                    WUNNISH, ROBIN

Judi said she would give it a try.

In the spring, we moved to Isle au Haut Judi and I,
Peter, Dawn, and Matthew, Maggie and Thunder, too, of
course.

On July 15, 1986, the Keeper's House Inn opened for
business.

GRANOLA FOR ROBIN

6 cups oats
1/2 cup whole wheat flour
1 cup wheat germ
1 cup sunflower seeds
1 cup pumpkin seeds
1 cup almond slices
1 cup sesame seeds
1/2 cup cashew pieces
1 cup raisins soaked in 1/2 cup warm water
3/4 cup oil
3/4 cup honey

Heat oil and honey. Pour over dry ingredients and mix. Spread mixture on three buttered cookie sheets and bake 1/2 hour at 275 degrees, stirring every 15 minutes. Five to ten minutes before done, add the drained cup of raisins. Serve with fresh fruit. Makes 3 1/2 quarts. Store in jars with tight lids. Judi suggests serving with cold skimmed milk, although Robin preferred using water (he boycotted the cattle and dairy industries because of their abuse of our nation's prairies).

2

THE STORYTELLER

June, July, and November 1986

"HE'S COMING! HE'S COMING! The well driller is here!" hollered Matthew, panting into the lighthouse kitchen, his thin chest heaving from the long run home. His excited face looked to me for approval, hoping his announcement would soothe my testy mood.

Even though our renovation work had gone smoothly since we bought the lighthouse station in April, the pressure of our impending opening was starting to get me down. Numbness dulling my senses, negativism, critical attitudes toward everyone and everything: I recognized these familiar symptoms of my recurrent depression. For me, the joy of rejuvenating the old buildings had become a string of oppressive and tedious chores. I'd managed to rough-in the plumbing and get a few bedrooms plastered, but on July fifteenth, our first guests would be arriving and things were nowhere near ready. The unfinished painting and the clutter from replacing rotten sills were bad enough, but the lack of running water could be ruinous for our soon-to-be opened inn. A drilled well was a necessity: another expensive, complicated problem on my overwhelming list of projects. And Judi was telling me not to worry!

I had made contact with a wandering well driller who roved the coast of Maine, sinking wells on mountaintops and ocean ledges. He promised to come to Isle au Haut. Arrangements were made to ferry his equipment over from Stonington, the trip contingent on the tides, the weather, the availability of a tug and barge. Mechanical breakdowns on the mainland and continuing spring storms created one delay after another, but with Matthew's announcement of his arrival, it seemed that finally we would have water.

An engine in low gear groaned from over the hill. We waited, amazed that any vehicle could climb the half mile of jagged path that reached here from the Town Road. A battered bumper then wedged its way between the trees and a four-wheel-drive pickup lurched into view, a tiny house trailer bouncing along behind. It grunted to a stop in the door yard.

Arched across the truck door, hand-painted letters read:

BRADLEY BURNS—MEDOMAK, MAINE
ARTESIAN WELLS

The driver swung open a makeshift plywood door and extruded himself. He was a stout man, thick with muscle. He wore a generic green suit of wrinkled work clothes, soiled with the dirt and oil of his trade. As he waded through our yard of unrestrained bayberry and beach grass, he detoured carefully around a patch of wild iris. With a broad, handsome grin, he raked his fingers through his curly hair and introduced himself.

"Name is Burns," he said. "You pick the spot, I poke the hole. Soon as I get situated, I'll go fetch my big lady— she's the workhorse in this outfit."

"I'm glad you're here," I said. "Time is short: we have
only a few days before our first guests arrive . . . I'm really
worried . . . I . . ."

"Slow down there, partner," he said, raising his hands in
protest. "We'll get you piped up in good shape. I've done
more urgent jobs than yours—lemme tell you about the
time I drilled down east in Machiaisport . . . nasty spot, it
was, high on the side of a hill. The land was owned by a
strange ol' bird, a duke from Turkey or some damn place . . .
heard he fled the Mediterranean with a gunboat of
mahogany trunks. Some says they was filled with . . ."

I couldn't listen to Bradley's ramblings: I was too pre-
occupied with my own concerns. I showed Bradley the site
we had selected near the house. Then Judi and I returned
to the kitchen to paint cabinets, occasionally watching from
the window to monitor his progress.

He puttered around the yard: gassing his generator,
hooking up a twisted antenna for his 12-volt TV, unloading
lengths of well casing and barrels of diesel fuel. Then he daw-
dled around the dwarfish trailer tidying his things, as if he had
all the time in the world, the freedom to do as he pleased. I
turned from the window and went back to my painting; no
time for idle spying—there was too much work to do!

That afternoon Bradley returned to the Town Landing
and drove back his drilling rig. A homemade contraption
welded to the frame of a '52 GM six-wheel-drive triple-
axle army truck, the mammoth machine lumbered through
the woods, leaving deep ruts and a wake of broken trees.
Decades of campaigns to the islands had left it crippled and
scarred, its sides dented and scraped bare of paint, the doors
long ago torn from their hinges and lost, the cab roof caved
in. It limped into place by the lighthouse.

Bradley spent the rest of the day setting up to drill.
With the agility of an acrobat, he scampered amid the rig-

ging of steel cables and hollow booms, adjusting fittings and connecting hydraulic hoses. As the sun set across the bay behind him, he threw the whining winches into gear and the massive tower lifted into the dusky sky like an awakening dinosaur.

Supper time. Bradley retired to his trailer to prepare his meal, inviting me along to socialize. He emptied two canvas bags of provisions, dropped a glob of butter in a hot skillet, started sautéing onions. While we discussed our hopes for the new well, he browned a pound of fatty hamburger, turning it frequently with a long-handled spoon, stirring in tomato paste, sauce, and pinches of oregano. Zesty aroma soon filled the air.

"It doesn't look like a drill," I said, peering through the doorway at the behemoth that rested in the shadows.

"Well, it ain't one of them fancy modern outfits," he said. "They could never get ashore here. Too big. Too heavy. Sure, they can drill a well hundreds of feet deep in a matter of hours, but you got to be a millionaire to buy one of them things—or drill a thousand wells a year to pay for it. No sir, I'd rather keep my ol' girl here, all paid for, you know. I can work if I want, go fishin' if I want, strike off for anywhere. I pick up the tough jobs the big boys leave behind." He chuckled. "That means I get to work the prettiest little corners on earth."

"Sounds like jobs might be few and far between," I said. "Couldn't you earn an easier living drilling wells for condominiums?"

"I ain't no workin' fool, Jeff," he said. "I want to grab hold of life while I can, enjoy the sunshine, take the time to swap a story."

Bradley ladled a spoon of grease from the simmering sauce and added it to his steaming spaghetti kettle, "to keep the noodles from sticking."

"Now, this ol' girl," he said, pointing through the door with the dripping spoon, "she's slow, but she don't stop." He paused, staring fondly at his homely but faithful machine. "She'll never stop. She'll pound away longer than I ever will."

Listening to Bradley, with his calm self-assurance and easy way, I felt the tension in my life begin to dissipate.

Bradley went on to explain how his brutish rig operated.

"This is what you call a 'tube and pounder,' it's not really a drill at all. The cable pulls a half-ton ram ten feet up the derrick, then lets her fall. BAM!" he barked, slamming a fist into the palm of his hand. "She just flails away at the earth, drivin' a hole in 'er belly, hour after hour, inch by inch, grinding the rock to dust."

"How do you get all the rubble out of the hole?" I asked.

"With that hollow boom hanging from the tower," he said, pointing through the shadows. "Now and then, I let off the ram and grab the tube, raise 'er up and let loose, burying 'er in the dust, like a kid picking up soda with a straw, with a finger stuck in the end so it don't slurp out."

While Bradley described the machine's functions, he acted out the movements with animated gestures, his strong, expressive hands knobby with calluses, disfigured with healed wounds.

"I suppose you have to be careful not to pinch your fingers," I said.

"See this gash?" he said, pointing to a scarred cleft across the back of his arm. "Got it while drilling the barrens in Washington County. Late at night. I'd just had supper and was curling up in my sack, when all of a sudden, this blood curdlin' howl erupts from the puckerbrush . . ."

I'm sure there was more to learn about well drilling, but I couldn't waste time listening to Bradley's stories that night—there weren't enough hours for all the chores that waited. At least I went to bed knowing there would be one less job to worry about: in a few days, cool clear water would be flowing through newly installed pipes.

The spaghetti? It wasn't too bad. I didn't finish it, though: the sauce coagulated in the bottom of my tin plate, a swirl of bloody paste and saturated fat, valve-clotting cholesterol.

IN THE MORNING, AS SOON AS THE SUN soaked through the eastern woods, the pounding started.

At first it was exciting to watch Bradley's machine peck away at the earth. It labored rhythmically, the diesel purring, the cables, booms, and gears working precisely together like an old team of draft horses. The well was being pounded right by the kitchen window, though, and after a few days the constant racket started to get on my nerves. We got no respite from the endless slamming and banging, the squeaky whirl of the wheels, the slap of steel cable against hollow boom, the constant drone of the diesel. Worst of all, the incessant pounding beat the bedrock like a Chinese water torture: "Donk . . . donk . . . donk . . . donk . . ." It gave me headaches, my sinuses clogged with the stench of diesel fuel, my body flinched with each deadening blow. It was driving me crazy!

"Donk . . . donk . . ."

It was all I could do to get through the day. I found projects in the boathouse, errands in town, trips off-island for supplies, anything to get away from the merciless noise. Late in the day, I crept tentatively back up the shore to reclaim my home. Bradley would see me coming and obligingly shut down the rig.

One afternoon, I returned from one of my off-island escapes and found Bradley standing by his pounder, hands on hips, staring into the hole.

"This rock is some wicked mean," he complained, wiping his brow with the back of an oily hand. "I've been poking holes in these islands for thirty years—never found a jag this hard."

I studied the messy opening. "How far has it gone?" I asked.

"Only twenty feet," he said.

It was less than a week till opening day. The virgin toilet bowls waited, shiny and dry. The pressure tanks stood empty in the corner of the cellar, the bright copper pipe ready to rush water to the kitchen pantry, for brewing coffee, for brushing our teeth, for nourishing the potted plants wilting in the entryway.

Although I enjoyed Bradley's company, his halting progress was just another cause for worry. I fussed with the decaying wiring in SweetiePie, my cantankerous 1951 Willys jeep salvaged from a friend's woodlot; I poked hopelessly at the rotten sills around the bulkhead; I had to splice five inches into period bed rails never meant to accommodate hotel-length mattresses; the forest of brush that crowded the buildings needed to be cleared away, too, so our soon-to-arrive guests could have an unobstructed ocean view. So much to do! But Bradley? He didn't worry about a thing. He only tended his hoary machine, giving her a squirt from the oil can now and then, or a twist of his wrench to keep her purring. How could he sail so smoothly in the midst of all this chaos?

Bradley kept me posted on his progress, usually filling in the details while he cooked his supper. He enjoyed housekeeping in his little hump of trailer, cooking his meals, visiting the village daily for provisions and a bit of storytelling. He tried to eat healthily, paying attention to the four food groups, but he didn't do it very well: his diet was predominantly packaged prepared foods laced with preservatives and hydrogenated fats. Sweets were irresistible. Whenever the fragrance of Judi's apple pie wafted from the kitchen window, his eyes became starry and he scurried to his trailer to fetch a saucer and fork.

During the last evenings before the inn opened, Brad and I became good friends. We sat on the back steps after dinner every night, watching the sun sink in the bay, me listening to his tales. We exchanged views on organic gardening, global politics, black holes in space, while he coaxed a shy doe from the woods, tossing her fragments of apple pie as she ventured nearer and nearer. One evening she took the crust from his hand.

And every morning the pounding resumed.

Facing up to the reality that the well wouldn't be ready till after we opened, we improvised a temporary plumbing system. I cleaned and patched the brick cisterns in the cellar and reconnected the downspouts to carry rainwater to fill them; the pantry pump then had a ready supply, so there was ample water for dishwashing and filling buckets for an outdoor shower. Judi would heat cistern water on the wood stoves for filling the antique pitchers in the guest rooms. We would lug drinking water from Sally's spring on the other side of the hill. Last but not least, the old outhouse that served generations of lighthouse keepers got a new coat of paint and a bouquet of wildflowers.

We opened on schedule.

MEANWHILE, BRADLEY CONTINUED TO POUND. Three days after the inn opened, he hit a tiny vein of water at sixty feet, not nearly enough for our needs. So, he kept on pounding.

During breakfast and dinner he courteously shut down the noisy rig, even though it meant taking longer to finish the job. We provisioned our guests with picnic lunches so they could spend the days exploring the shore or hiking the mountain trails, enabling the pounding to continue unabated during the daylight hours. Fortunately, the cacophonous machinery, the outhouse on the hill, the outdoor shower, somehow all these discomforts coalesced into an appealing frontier ambiance.

But the strongest antidote to the inconvenience was Bradley Burns himself: guests found him irresistible, his little gypsy encampment curious and intriguing. When they returned late in the afternoon from their treks, they gathered around to ask about his trade and hear about his life migrating between the islands. He shut down the pounder and sat on the heaved-up pile of dirt by the hole, his sleeves rolled up, his eyes bulging with enthusiasm. His stories flowed profusely: accounts of drilling on distant isles, tales of danger on the sea. His bandaged index finger jabbed the sky to accent a point while the sun slithered toward the horizon behind him.

"Why, one time years back," he would say, "I was poundin' a well off the Bay of Fundy . . . burnt out three carbide points tryin' to crack the bedrock . . . nasty stuff it was, so gawdawful hard she went burrowin' sideways and twisted the ram in knots . . ."

Or . . .

"Russ Devereux barged me off Friendship Island one November during a hellacious gale—seas heaved so wicked fierce the peanut butter rolled right off my toast . . ."

IT WAS THE END OF JULY WHEN BRADLEY summoned me for a final report.

"Done the best I can," he said. "We've only found that one little vein, but saltwater could infiltrate if we go any deeper," he conjectured, nodding at the ocean lapping at the shore less than fifty feet from our door. "You got a hole, a reservoir, 180 feet deep; that's enough to hold a good supply. She'll fill up at night, and drain down during the day when you're drawin' on 'er."

The next day I had the pump installed and connected to the generator. I cranked 'er up, opened all the water valves, threw the circuit breaker: the welcome liquid erupted through the copper arteries, flooding the flush tanks and water heaters. Finally, the ambrosia of life had arrived to quench our thirst and cleanse our bodies and poach our eggs. And for the first time in its existence, the old house heard the sound of a flushing john.

DURING HIS TIME AT THE LIGHTHOUSE, six other islanders had asked Bradley to pound wells, so I saw him frequently during the rest of the summer. No matter how busy he was, he always found time to stop and gab at the store, to tell a story and share some laughter. On Saturday nights he appeared at the square dances in the Town Hall, or at the card games in Billy's shop, or I might see him in the evening, lingering in the mist of the floodlight on the Town Landing, watching the kids land mackerel—and I could always find him wherever an apple pie was baking.

Late in the year, Bradley was finishing his last well over on Sheep Thief Gulch. He ran the rig late into the night (no summer folks left to complain about the noise). Time was getting short; soon, stormy weather would force him to leave the island.

Brian McCorrison, one of the few people still on the east side that late in the year, stopped daily to chat with Bradley. One cold November night, Brian woke several times, aware of the rig banging away in the blackness. In the morning, he went to see if Bradley had stayed up in a last feverish effort to finish. He found the pounder running smoothly.

"Donk . . . donk . . . donk . . . donk . . ."

But Bradley Burns no longer tended his mechanical friend; he lay sprawled motionless in a bed of scarlet autumn blueberry bushes, his boots still laced tight.

"Donk . . . donk . . . ," went Bradley's pounding machine. The slow cadence of her blows echoing along the shore, she stood among the mourning rings of spruce and stone and kept right on working.

I LEARNED A LOT ABOUT ISLAND LIVING during my first summer on Isle au Haut. I learned how to rig an outhaul to hold my skiff, how to feel with the ball of my foot to find clams hiding in the mud flat, how to fell a spruce tree without my chainsaw binding. As the inn grew and the problems became more numerous and daunting, the logistics and maintenance more tiring, the obscure requests of guests too crazy and overwhelming, I realized I learned my most important lesson from Bradley Burns.

"Enjoy life while you can," he said. "And never forget to take the time to tell a story."

JUDI'S PERFECT APPLE PIE

Pies are special when they are baked in a scrumptious piecrust. To me, the piecrust is what makes the pie. I never use anything but Crisco when I make my crust. But the real secret to perfect crust, in my opinion, is to handle the dough as little as possible. Sometimes, my pies don't look as beautiful as the ones in the super-

market freezer, but that's because I refuse to roll out a
crust a second time, even if the dough is falling apart.
Just piece it back together and put it in the pie plate
as best you can.

—Judi Burke, from her cookbook *Kitchen with a View*

FOR THE CRUST:
1 1/3 cups white flour, sifted
1 tsp. salt
2/3 cup Crisco
1/3 cup cold water

Combine flour and salt in medium bowl. Cut in Crisco with two knives to
size of peas. Add cold water. Mix only enough so that you can roll out two
crusts on a board, well floured to prevent the dough from sticking.

FOR THE PIE:
8 cooking apples
1/4 cup white sugar
1/4 cup brown sugar
1/2 tsp. cinnamon
1/8 tsp. nutmeg
6 dabs butter
milk

Roll out bottom crust and place in 9-inch pie pan. Peel, core, and slice
apples. Place them piled high into pan. Sprinkle combined sugars, cinnamon, and nutmeg over apples. Dab with butter. Roll out and cover with
top crust. Sprinkle top with milk. Bake at 450 degrees for 10 minutes, then
at 350 degrees for 25 minutes. Serve warm. Maybe add a little scoop of
vanilla ice cream?

3

THE CHAIR

July 23, 1986

SOON AFTER WE MOVED into the lighthouse station, I
learned the first rule of island living: there is always a use
for everything. Here there are no shopping malls or hardware stores, no telephones or mail carriers, no delivery vans
to materialize through the fog with a coil of rope or a
pound of nails. Every piece of old machinery and every
length of rusty pipe must be saved and cherished, for at any
moment some archaic remnant may be called upon to save
the day.

One of my first tasks was to organize the junk in the
barn and the boathouse. It took days to sort through the sea
chests and wooden crates. I glued broken balusters and
returned them to the front porch, refinished interior doors
and hung them, patched cistern downspouts and wired
them in place so rainwater once again flowed from the roof
to the brick reservoir in the cellar.

Not everything I found was hard and
mechanical. Some of the old furniture was
a softer, more soulful reminder of the past:
a side chair with a rose embroidered on its
worn cushion, an iron bed with a sagging
mattress, dressers whose drawers were

filled with creased photographs and old diaries. Heaps of the old furniture were everywhere, disjointed and scarred, with broken spindles jutting from the piles like bleached ribs in an elephant graveyard. Peter and I spent weeks gluing, sanding, and painting. Finally, one by one, the rooms began to blossom, each one attracting a perfect combination of freshly painted pieces. Every item found its proper place, its intended use.

Except for one. It was a rocker upholstered in brown vinyl. Old, maybe fifty years or more. Squarish. Rigid. And ugly, just plain ugly. Paint and polish could help it no more than the cosmetics of an undertaker primping a corpse for burial. Its pointed rockers jutted up at an angle designed to gash the shins of those who strayed too close, and its plastic upholstery was the color of Maine mud in late March. Torn badly on one side, the fake leather gaped like a horrid wound, exposing swaths of stuffing that appeared to be decaying hair from some prehistoric beast. Although ripped and tattered, the material showed none of the wear patterns usually found on old furniture; apparently, no one had ever sat in it! Like a feared leper, the chair must have been locked away in dusty attics for its entire life.

I tried to find a place for it, I really did. I tried it in every room of the house, on the porch and even in the kitchen. But in each place I tried, its vile nature seemed only to grow, as if the chair were taking on a life of its own. It threatened the ambiance of our fledgling inn, the safety of our guests, and our budding reputation as fine innkeepers. It would have to go.

I posted a notice in the Island Store:

FREE: NICE ROCKING CHAIR
SEE IT AT THE LIGHTHOUSE

Several families scheduled interviews. I waited nervously while Judi baked blueberry muffins and brewed a pot of her favorite Colombian-Sumatran blend.

Leland Small was the first to arrive. On his way back into the harbor from hauling lobster traps, he dropped anchor and skiffed ashore. I had the chair sitting there just inside the boathouse door, its rockers polished, its vinyl skin waxed and gleaming in the bright July sunshine. The torn side faced the wall, and I made sure the most glaring deformity wouldn't be noticed: a strip of duct tape bound the wound and kept the innards from spilling out.

Lee greeted me, then paced back and forth in front of the chair, eyeing it uncomfortably. He twisted the ends of his coarse red mustache, searching for the right words. A gentle fellow, he finally built up the courage to deliver the verdict.

"Well, Jeff, I just need something for the shop, where I can sit and knit bait bags and such—nothing fancy, of course—but to tell you the truth, that's got to be the ugliest damn chair I've ever seen!"

"Well, yes, it doesn't look like a very good chair," I admitted. "But this here chair is unique. You could use it for lots of things: rocking Mary's baby to sleep, a sawbuck for holding lobster traps while you repair them. How about kindling for stoking your stoves?"

"Nope," said Lee. "That chair reeks of trouble: I wouldn't even set my chainsaw down on that dreadful thing!"

He didn't wait for the muffins and coffee. He was so eager to get away he almost forgot to loop his skiff's painter around the stern cleat. As he pulled free of the rocks, he glanced back suspiciously, as if he expected to see me hefting the cursed chair down through the ledges in an attempt to toss it aboard.

Several other folks came to look at the chair, but the results were always the same (it doesn't take long for the word to get around). After that, of course, there were no more interested parties. A few curious kids from the village did come to gawk, as if it were some deformed creature in a circus sideshow.

I was getting desperate. Memories of our years in Pemaquid came to mind: I remembered our Nubian goat, Florence. She broke a leg one winter and I had to ask my brother to put the poor thing down. Now again, I asked a few of my new island friends to take this albatross off my hands, pleading for help with a quandary I couldn't solve alone. But they only smiled, snickered, found ways to avoid me.

I paced the boathouse, glaring at the chair. Drastic measures were needed.

Fire! A fine choice! I could gore the vinyl with a broken oar and fling the rocker into a blazing brush pile. But the burning vinyl might give off black noxious smoke, polluting the atmosphere and calling attention to my failure to find a use for the chair. That would never do.

Drowning was another possibility. I could weigh it down with chimney blocks, drag it down to the shore on a moonless night, and dump it overboard. But with my luck a scallop dragger would haul it up and toss it back on our shore: after all, by now the entire world knew where the ugliest chair in Maine belonged.

I could bury it alive—that would be a kick! It would be difficult, though: around the lighthouse there is no soil, only granite boulders and volcanic ledge. It's easy digging in the gravel pit, but getting the awkward chair over to the east side without being seen would be tricky. And even if I succeeded, chances are that sooner or later someone excavating for sand would come upon the remains. There would be no doubt who the culprit was.

Since none of the traditional techniques would do, something more creative was needed, I thought, leaning

against the workbench and glaring at the chair. I could tie
a pair of deer antlers on the chair and hide it in the woods
near the shore; doubtless there would be a boat of poach-
ers in the fall who would spot the horns and blow the das-
tardly thing to smithereens. Or perhaps I could lash an outboard motor to the back and send it skating across the
water on its ski-like rockers, to meet its fate running
aground on some distant ledge—or being eaten by sharks!
But with all its high-tech equipment, the Coast Guard
would probably come to its rescue and the media would
pick up the story:

COAST GUARD CAPTURES
HIGH-SPEED VINYL CHAIR

Once photos were released, the chair would be instantly
identified and I would be apprehended.

PHANTOM CHAIR TRACED TO ISLAND—
INNKEEPER CHARGED WITH FAILURE
TO FIND USE FOR PERFECTLY GOOD ITEM

I would appeal, of course. But my career would be
ruined and I would be forced to sell the station to cover
legal expenses. There would be nothing left to live for,
everything I worked so hard for all these years lost. My
friends would desert me. Judi would find solace with a
more successful man. Shamed to tears, the kids would turn
away from me. Even Maggie would slink away the first
chance she got, indignant over the sparse pickings as we
bummed from town to town, sleeping in bus stations and
begging handouts on street corners.

My head reeled with the consequences. I became dizzy,
hot, faint. My knees began to tremble, my stomach filled

with lead. The world around me became hazy, the boathouse floor began to roll beneath my feet. Then, like an anesthetized animal, I began to slump, and, as I faltered, my hands groped for anything stable—and I collapsed . . . into . . . the chair.

For a few moments I lay recovering, the chair rocking gently from the impact. It had been soft enough to cushion my fall, yet solid enough not to buckle.

I waited. I felt a little better, a little stronger. The dizzying gyrations in my head began to ease. The chair cradled me in its soft lap, the way my mother did when I was a little boy, and the cushions began to absorb my anxiety. I pushed gently against the floor. The chair responded, rocking softly. I pushed a bit more firmly and the chair surged, instantaneously, like a fine racehorse reacting to its jockey's urgings. The smooth faded vinyl was warm from the afternoon sun, sensuous and alive to my touch, and the rockers creaked a pleasant lullaby that soothed my frazzled nerves. I closed my eyes and rocked.

TODAY THAT ONCE-DESPISED HULK of hardwood, hair, and plastic still sits by the boathouse door, positioned just right so I can gaze southwest out to Saddleback Ledge. I come here to find a moment of serenity, a taste of peace, a chance to dwell a bit with the Island Spirit. When I am here, I am never alone. My chair by the boathouse door has become my friend and confidant—and a reminder to me that there is always a use for everything, even things that are as ugly as sin.

DOWNEAST BLUEBERRY
MUFFINS

I cup white flour
I cup whole wheat flour
1/2 cup sugar
I Tbs. baking powder
1/2 tsp. salt
1/2 tsp. cinnamon
1/2 cup butter
1/2 cup milk
2 eggs
1/2 tsp. vanilla
1 1/2 cups blueberries

Combine dry ingredients in a bowl. Melt butter. After butter has cooled slightly, stir in milk, then eggs and vanilla. Add egg mixture to dry ingredients. Stir only until well moistened. Stir in berries. Spoon batter into greased 12-cup muffin tin. Sprinkle with sugar. Bake 15 minutes at 375 degrees. Just as tasty if you use raspberries or peaches!

4

DOWSING FOR THE CAT

Mid-August 1986

DOWSING, I HAD ALWAYS HEARD, is a method to find water. Holding a forked apple stick, a skilled dowser need only walk across a plot of land to find out whether water lies below; tugs and pulls of the stick lead the dowser along, the end of the stick suddenly dipping downward like a pointing index finger when a vein is detected. The practice has its skeptics, of course, folks who claim it isn't scientific, that it doesn't work. But I grew up a believer in flying saucers and the Ouija board, so dowsing always made sense to me. It wasn't until recently, however, that I learned this ancient art can lead to more than water.

Grace taught me all about it. A longtime friend and an excellent cook, she helped us get the inn established. Leaving her job at the Grainery Health Food Coop on the mainland, she came to the lighthouse several days a week so Judi could have a rest from the kitchen.

One sunny August morning, I jump-started my Jeep, SweetiePie, and drove down to the Town Landing to meet her. She waved unabashedly as *Mink* pulled in, her long black hair bouncing on her shoulders, huge round eyeglasses cover-

35

ing half her pretty face. Dressed in her usual outfit of plain
clothes and exotic jewelry, she climbed the gangway, her
hearty laughter a welcome greeting. She carried her familiar khaki knapsack bulging with New Age books, a change
of clothes, and the eccentric little tokens and talismans that
are so much a part of her life. But on this trip Grace had
brought more than just a knapsack: under each arm she
clutched a large vented box. Apprehension tainted her
smile.

After a barrage of explanations, she opened the boxes
and set free her feline friends, Liza and Fred, who crawled
all over me while I jostled SweetiePie hurriedly back to
the lighthouse (I'm allergic to cats). Grace claimed she suf-
fered emotional hardship when she was separated from
them, so she couldn't leave them behind on the mainland.
And besides, she explained, they would love it at the lighthouse.

They certainly did. It wasn't long before they took
over. Fred was the homebody, content to lounge on the
back porch and be fondled and fussed over by guests. He
never strayed far from the mound of organic cat food Grace
left heaped in an old cake pan.

Liza, on the other hand, was a hunter. With a thirst for
adventure, she prowled the forest day and night, terrorizing
the red squirrels that screamed from the spruce boughs.
They could elude her, leaping from tree to tree in a dazzling display of acrobatics, but they were pushed farther and
farther from the inn by her pursuits. Not so lucky were the
white-footed mice and pine voles; confined to earth, they
were no match for her persistent stalking and insatiable
appetite.

Every day Liza's hunting trips grew longer. Finally the
inevitable happened: Grace had to get back to her job on
the mainland and Liza hadn't returned. She had no choice

but to go without her, climbing aboard the mailboat with Fred in one box and leaving the other behind with a six-pack of organic cat food.

During the five days Grace was gone, Liza never came back. When I gave Grace the bad news on her return, she became visibly depressed. She stumbled about the kitchen, lost in thought, making too much ratatouille and overbaking her croissants. After supper she went on a long walk searching for Liza. I heard her calls echo through the night, her voice laced with desperation.

The next morning I came into the kitchen for my first cup of decaf. The room was smoky with overcooked food: burned peach muffins, coffee percolated too long, scorched blueberry pancakes forgotten on the griddle. Our friend Heather, an island resident who waits table here, rushed back and forth to the dining room with platters of dried-out grub, stumbling over Maggie, who lay slumbering in front of the stove.

In the midst of all the chaos stood Grace, oblivious to the ruckus. She would flip a few smoking pancakes, then lean over a trail guide unfolded on the table. Above the map dangled her Subaru key, suspended from her outstretched hand on a rawhide boot string. The key twisted and swung in tiny little arcs.

I worried about the service.

"What are you up to, Grace? Looking for gold?" I said, hoping to bring her back.

"No, Jeff," she said, pausing to pencil a few x's on the map. "I'm dowsing for Liza."

Inch by inch, the ghostly key coaxed her hand around the map, twisting slightly as it passed over the contour lines of Bald Mountain.

"You just let the key drift along until it tells you where Liza is?" I said. I knew Grace used this method to locate rare herbs and to site wells. But cats? (I became so fascinated, I forgot about the guests.)

"Well, it isn't easy," she said. "I have to concentrate, really concentrate It might guide me to the general area, you know, somewhere to start. It isn't working, though . . . I'm too tired, and too distraught."

Heather stood in the mudroom, fanning the back door to force out residual smoke. Maggie stirred to life when I started to fill her bowl, bounding across the room and knocking over a chair. Mr. Flowers, our guest in the Horizon Room, came in looking for seconds on orange juice.

"How do you actually do it, Gracie?" I asked. "I mean, what does it *feel* like?"

She relaxed a bit and sat down at the kitchen table. "Think of your dowsing medium as a taproot into your soul," she said, pushing aside the butter dish so it wouldn't obstruct the space between us. "It's a tool to generate messages from power sources in our bodies and in the air and earth around us. You must believe. You must be at one with your medium. Each dip, each twist, each little tug has a connection to What Is Meant to Be."

"But Grace, using a key over a map, isn't that a bit vague?"

She was a locomotive now, steaming along on renewed enthusiasm. "Beginnings, Jeff, beginnings. It gives me a reference point, that's all. Remember: the discovery of any lost treasure begins with finding a scrap of faded parchment or an arrow carved in stone. And besides, dangling a key is a rather specialized method. For beginners, those with the will and the calling, I recommend apprenticing with **L** rods."

Her gray eyes were now afire, focused into mine. "Want to try?" she asked.

"Sure," I said.

My imagination ran wild: what a thrill, tromping around the island, geysers bursting from the earth wherever I go, sweet cold springs that would make Bradley Burns proud of me. I could also use the buggers to find pockets of gravel to improve my road, and jettisoned schooner anchors in shallow coves, and Cheryl Proctor's lost earring . . . maybe even oil!

"You need heavy wire," Grace began. "It has to be straight—the straighter, the better. You need two pieces. Bend them into right angles, one side ten inches long, the other side five inches."

Grace rose and stood squarely on the kitchen floor, lifting her arms perpendicular to her body, shifting her weight from one foot to the other, like a shortstop digging in. "You hold them like this, like two pistols," she said, curling her fingers around imaginary steel. "Hold them parallel to the ground, but hold them loosely. They must be able to rotate, to drift at will, to swing and search."

I stood opposite her, mirroring her movements. I could almost feel the wire pulsing in my palms.

"Concentration is everything," she continued. "Establish a set of signals. If they cross, that can mean one thing. If they swing apart, another. You must be clear about what you want to know and how you want the indications conveyed. Then, let them take you to What Is Meant to Be."

As she finished her demonstration, the fire drained from her eyes, and the excitement in her voice waned, too. She was exhausted from worrying. She tucked an avocado and havarti sandwich into her day pack, wandered out the back door, and traipsed gloomily toward Bald Mountain, hoping she might find some sign of Liza.

I lost no time. Disregarding my daily chores, I rushed down to the boathouse. I rummaged through nail kegs

filled with broken boat parts and searched among piles of
fishing gear. It didn't take long to find what I was after.

It was a twisted coil of rusty wire. I had found it our
first week here, buried in the spring grass by the woodshed.
At the time it seemed silly to save it. There were only a few
yards and it was so kinked and so corroded that scales
crumbled off in my hands, exposing a surface pockmarked
as coarsely as the moon. There had been something singu-
lar about it, though, something special that made it more
than junk. Maybe it was the way it lay intertwined with
the grass, or its rich earthy color—it seemed to grow from
the clay, a product of time and toil. Someday it would
be needed again, I thought, so I had stored it in the
boathouse.

Now, I stretched it out on the workbench. I cut two
rough lengths. Using a ball-peen hammer, I started working one on the anvil.

"Tap, tap, tap."

The hammer fell on the soft metal, flattening the
humps and kinks. I turned it slowly, pausing every few raps,
sighting down the wire to find its aberrations.

"Tap, tap, tap."

Swaths of sunlight filtered through the dusty window
panes, illuminating the creation taking form in my hands.
The hammer fell rhythmically, each gentle rap giving rise
to a puff of orange dust set afire by the rays of sun. My
hands worked effortlessly, automatically. Inch by inch, the
wire moved across the anvil, exposing its imperfections to
the hammer's caress.

"Tap, tap, tap."

The wire grew warm and responsive, as if a tiny heart
inside was responding to my manipulations. The more I
tapped, the more it asked to be turned and smoothed, fondled and perfected.

I forged the second wire, then clamped them both in the vise and carefully bent them to form right angles. With a pair of diagonal cutters, I finished the job, snipping the legs to the lengths Grace had specified.

Then I experimented with the swing of the rods in my hands. They arced freely, tingling against my palms. Moment by moment, this feeling intensified. These were not just cold iron! They felt alive, as though the blood in my veins surged through them, as though my sensory perceptions had grown outward, like the feelers of a lobster or the radar of a bat! They directed me, pulled me, led me from the darkness of the boathouse into the summer light.

The sky wrapped me in warmth. A soaring seagull squawked salutations, blueberry bushes whispered, and a crowd of faces watched from the clouds. I moved through the trees and along the shore to the lighthouse, mysteriously drawn by the dowsing rods that grew from my hands.

"Should I be looking for water?" I asked, not knowing from where to expect an answer.

Nothing.

"Can I harness this power to solve the mysteries of life?" I pondered. "To enrich myself? To live forever?"

Nothing.

Only the breeze spoke. And the slosh of the sea.

Then I remembered what Grace had said. "Focus. Focus your energy," her words came back to me. "Be in unity with your rods—then you'll find What Is Meant to Be."

So I planted my feet and concentrated. My brow furrowed deep, my breathing slowed, the sweat broke out on my neck. Then, it all became clear to me . . . and the rods began to tremble . . . and shake . . . and heave . . . focused on the edge of the woods. Suddenly the wire jerked and the high grass bounding the woods whipped open—and there was Liza! Wild and haggard, she flew into the clearing with a loud, hungry cry, yanked from the forest back to where she belonged.

Grace was jubilant.

That night she prepared a banquet: fresh mushroom soup, garden salad with a curry Chablis dressing, hot-from-the-oven lemon yogurt muffins, a savory Crab Imperial with broccoli in an almond sauce, and baked potatoes with sour cream and chives. For dessert she presented a fruit torte and a double chocolate cheesecake. After the guests had been fed, there was plenty left over for the rest of us. We sat around the kitchen late that night, rejoicing in Liza's return.

THE DOWSING RODS? I'VE GOT THEM STILL. After we finished our meal that night and the others had all gone to bed, I took a walk down to the boathouse. There I lit a candle. In the soft glow were the anvil and hammer, the vise and snips, midwives to my creation. Above the workbench, I hung the rods on a wooden peg. Mere rusty wire, that's all they are, without the human touch to give them heart. So, they wait on the peg: they'll be called into service another time for What Is Meant to Be, when the conditions are proper, the will is there, and the cause is as noble as finding Gracie's cat.

GRACE'S SPICY
MUSHROOM SOUP

4 Tbs. butter
2 cups chopped onions
salt
3/4 pound mushrooms, sliced
1 Tbs. minced fresh dill weed or 1 tsp. dried dill weed
2 cups chicken broth
1 Tbs. tamari
1 1/2 tsp. hot Hungarian paprika
3 Tbs. flour
1 cup milk
pepper
2 tsp. fresh lemon juice
1/4 cup sour cream
parsley garnish

In a saucepan, sauté onions in 2 tablespoons butter until soft but not brown. Sprinkle lightly with salt. Add mushrooms, dill weed, 1/2 cup broth, tamari, and paprika. Cover pot and simmer 15 minutes. Heat remaining 2 tablespoons butter in large saucepan. Whisk in flour and cook, stirring until mixture foams. Remove from heat. Add the milk all at once and whisk vigorously to blend well. Return to heat and continue to whisk until sauce is smooth (5 minutes). Stir in mushroom mixture and remaining broth. Cover pot. Simmer 15 to 20 minutes. Just before serving, gently stir in sour cream and lemon juice. Top with parsley garnish. Serves 8.

THE BOAT LANDING—PART I
Jeffrey Gets His Feet Wet

Summer–Fall 1986

BACK DURING THE DECADES when the lighthouse station was manned, the keepers used a marine railway to haul their freight ashore. The remains of the decaying trolley still lie beached on the rocks and the last scales of iron track bleed rust on the boathouse floor, but the timber rails that ran down into the water rotted away long before we arrived. It must have been risky getting ashore, with the tide, the wind, and the weather all conspiring to make landing dangerous.

A clumsy keeper could have paid dearly if he ever stumbled: the rocks are slippery, the tides rise quickly, and the sea is unforgivingly cold because the Georges Banks steer the warm Gulf Stream straight up to the Canadian Maritimes, leaving the deep, protected belly of Isle au Haut Bay filled with frigid water—even in mid-summer. I often wondered why the Lighthouse Service hadn't ever built a pier.

With a full-service inn to supply, we needed a reliable landing. The Keeper's House required frequent shipments of lobster, flounder, and clams, butter and eggs, a variety of exotic

cheeses every week, and coffee freshly ground. And what
about all the sheets and towels that had to be laundered in
Stonington, and the concrete, hardware, and lumber to
continue our renovations? And what about the guests?
They had to be transported, too—we couldn't expect them
to wade ashore from the mailboat: the water's too cold, the
slimy rocks are crawling with crabs and jellyfish. I'd have to
build a deep-water pier, where *Mink* could dock on any
tide. In the meantime, I'd need to get supplies ashore some
other way.

When we first arrived in the spring, I met Bones
McDonnell in Stonington. Equipped with *Nana*, his lobster
boat, a Jeep on the island, a plethora of seaman's and car-
penter's skills, an ingenious mind, playful blue eyes, and a
droopy mustache that bristled in the wind, he was the perfect fellow to help me erect a temporary high-tide landing
platform, a place where we could off-load building materials and supplies. We built a primitive structure, fashioned of
logs and slabs from the island sawmill, lashed together with
pot warp and wire. Little more than a platform on stilts, it
clung to the bedrock near the high-tide line. Bones would
wait for high water, then scoot *Nana* in, tying her fore and
aft, and we would rush to unload plywood and two-by-
fours before the water turned. It got us by while I planned
a more sophisticated structure.

There had always been piers along the Thorofare in
more protected places: at the Town Landing, the Island
Store, the Point Lookout Club. Some of the fishermen have
them, too, gangly thatches of pilings crisscrossed with
planks and piled with fishing gear. Of course, here at the
lighthouse we lacked the protection of the harbor, but to
me it didn't matter (the bay seemed gentle enough). Still, I
thought I should get an experienced opinion. I decided to
visit Billy and Bernadine, my neighbors around the cove.

Every day Billy circles *Islander* in front of the lighthouse, hauling his traps and moving his lines. He is a descendant of Pelatia Barter, Isle au Haut's first year-round settler two hundred years ago. For ten generations Billy's kin have steamed past here, harvesting lobster and fish. They know the seas, the tides, the shores. They predict the weather from the pattern of clouds, the mood of the bay as the seasons turn. They've lived through the tempests, too, and seen the punishment they can give. In the evenings, after a long day of hauling traps, Billy trods home and collapses in his La-Z-Boy recliner. Between his stocking feet, he watches the sun sink behind Kimball Head, the shimmer of water where mackerel run, the old fish weir that rots between the tides. He watches the lighthouse, too.

Late one afternoon, I clattered across the cobble beach to Billy's. It was one of those eerie silent evenings when the slightest surge of water or distant cawing crow seems to be right beside you. The tide was low and the wind had fallen out. The sun hovered near the horizon. A pair of loons drifted near the shore, dark and massive as battleships, their sorrowful moaning echoing across the still evening water.

I climbed up the bank, skirted the house, knocked on the door. Inside, Bernie's retriever, Amber, let out a warning howl. The TV was blasting, too, jabbering sitcoms and commercials. From somewhere else inside, Billy's VHF chattered with the voices of local fishermen discussing the day's catch or gossiping about the fancy charter sloop that ran aground on Osprey Ledge. The clanking of pots told me dinnertime was near.

"Amber, what's the matter with you?" Bernadine's scolding voice rose above the tumult. "It's only Jeff outside. Come on in, Jeff, come on in."

I shoved open the screen door and entered the mudroom, stepping around Billy's fishing boots to gain access to

the kitchen. Greeting me were a friendly smile and the
aroma of sizzling pork.

"Sit right down—we're just about to eat," said Bernie.
She scooted around the kitchen, straining a pot of boiled
potatoes, lifting the lid of another steaming cauldron to
inspect the progress inside.

"Hi Bernie. Hi Billy," I said, even though I couldn't see
much of him: his legs stretched across the doorway between
the kitchen and living room, his stocking feet propped up
while the rest of Billy lounged out of sight in his recliner.

"'Lo," said invisible Billy, from the other side of the
wall.

Bernadine pushed a plate in front of me and ordered
me to eat.

"Corned hake . . . with all the trimmings, that's what
were having for supper," she said. "Billy caught it yesterday
in one of his lobster traps out by the Seal Ledges."

Bernadine's voice dances like music, accompanied by
the tinkle of earring bells that jingle with her laughter. Her
bright curly hair and rosy cheeks always cheer me up, and
her wardrobe of Spanish leather belts and hand-painted
cowboy boots provides a spicy contrast to the usual island
attire of flannel shirts and baseball caps.

Billy appeared in the doorway, looking hungry, and
pulled up a chair. Bernie brought platter after platter, cov-
ering the tablecloth until there was hardly space left for
elbows: mounds of flaky corned hake, saucers of crispy pork
tidbits, a cup of renderings from the frying pan to ladle over
the fish, bowls of cooked onions, boiled potatoes, turnips,
and squash.

After my third helping, I asked Billy for his opinion on
building a pier at the lighthouse.

"Hard place to keep a pier, I'd guess," he said. "Of
course, the old station used the rail tram, with the whole

works pinned hard to the ledges. No target exposed to the storms that way. I guess the seas rolled right over 'em." In his callused hand, Billy's dinner fork poked at the last flakes of fish, pressing them between the tines.

"I'd rather build a pier," I said, "with a floating dock where Buster can tie up, and a thirty-foot ramp to reach between them. That's comin' and goin' in style."

"Might be a bit exposed there on the Point," said Billy.

"But Billy, SweetiePie is already falling apart running back and forth to town, and we're not even busy yet!" I said. "By next year we'll be overflowing with guests and dirty laundry. We *need* a boat landing."

"Well, it would be handy," said Billy with a doubtful look.

"And I'd have a place to tie a skiff, a little motorboat to fetch the mail and take our guests for rides. Without a pier we're land-bound. Don't you agree?"

"I guess so," said Billy. "I s'pose you could get Russ Devereaux to build you one—he can do 'most anything. She might take a lickin' in the winter, when the nor'westers start to pound. Never been one there before, but it might be worth a try . . . anyway . . . I s'pose."

DURING THAT SUMMER OF '86, Billy hauled his traps in the Thorofare and watched Russell Devereaux build our pier. Tugboats and barges, compressors and cranes, Russ had a flotilla anchored by the lighthouse, and the fireworks of his welders burned late into the night, taking advantage of a rare drain tide. Soon, the gaunt steel beams rose from the ledges, their legs spread wide to resist the tackling seas, their feet gripped to the rock with steel pins driven two feet deep. Billy witnessed the whole affair, then saw the mail-boat's virgin landing here. He watched askance while our

guests struggled up the ramp and came ashore, toting their
backpacks and fishing gear.

From the time Russ had the pier completed, our lives
were simplified. No more jarring rides in SweetiePie back
and forth to town; now the mailboat could bring our guests
directly to the lighthouse. Bones's old landing platform
became a place where only seagulls gathered.

The late-afternoon arrival of *Mink* became the focus of
my day. After Buster unloads our guests, they climb the
ramp to the pier. I wait in the boathouse. With my tattered
plaid shirt and my Ocean Spray baseball cap, I strike a pose,
caulking *Alma*'s bottom. I greet them warmly, the way a
good host should. They regard me curiously, eager to know
my story, assuming I am some old salt born and bred by the
sea. But I cannot tell a lie: the sea is a mystery to me; I can't
even tie a bowline; I grew up in Columbus, Ohio, I tell
them, I'm just a runaway, a refugee from the Big Ten. Good
fortune is all that brings me here, and it's only the existence
of this landing that allows me to survive, this wood and
metal contraption that adjusts to the tides, my umbilical
cord to the rest of the world.

All during our maiden year we reveled in the glory of
our new boat landing. It all seemed so simple then, the
peaceful, safe, lazy days of summer passing one by one, all
made easy by this magical connecting link where our visitors
came and left, groceries too, and tanks of propane gas, banana
boxes layered with laundered sheets, lumber from Deer Isle,
parts for SweetiePie, everything we needed delivered to our
door. I inquired about insurance for the new pier, but my
agent only grimaced, complained about the risky open water
here, and referred me to Lloyd's of London. Aware of their
notoriously high rates, I never bothered to apply.

Then the first nor'wester hit. It came late on a mid-
September afternoon, only two months after the new pier

had been completed. I stood in the boathouse and watched the rain blown sideways, the huge seas barreling in, heathen monsters foreign to me. They curled around the Point and pounded the shore, each rumbling swell a gasp higher than the one before. And there was still an hour more of tide to rise.

Although the new steel pier stood four feet above the seas, the old homemade landing platform that Bones had built was soon submerged in froth. The wrecking waves worked to shake it loose. Eventually, its grip to the rock let go and it lurched to the surface, thrashing. The crashing seas heaved it against the rocks, splintering and breaking timbers, then sucked it back in the undertow, then hurled it once again.

The largest chunk, a section of platform still lashed to an upright piling, washed underneath the new pier and became trapped there between the carrying beams. With each arriving wave, the piling rose and fell, a menacing battering ram.

"*Whunk!*" The piling pounded the new pier's underbelly. With every passing minute, with every inch of rising tide, the force of the beating mounted.

"*Skreeak!*" A plank on the pier pried loose.

"*Whaaaang!*" The hand rail shook.

Then, a brutal rogue wave came from out of nowhere, coursing in, heaving the platform upward. The protruding piling rose unmercifully and burst through the decking. The sound of shattering timber crackled through the storm.

I was terrified. My placid summer bay had gone berserk, the sea transformed to a horrific force. The howling skies, the thundering roar, the mountains of water that crashed ashore—I felt like the target of a bombing attack, shell-shocked, unable to act. My brand new pier of welded

steel and treated timber was being demolished. What could
I do? Isn't this a job for the Coast Guard? The Army Corps
of Engineers? Red Adair? God? But there were no helping
hands anywhere in sight—not even a late-season, bargain-
hunting, foliage-seeking tourist had braved this storm to
visit the island. Peter and Dawn were away at college. Even
Judi was gone, off in town with Matthew for Parent-
Teacher Night.

The battering ram rose again; another plank went flying. I couldn't bear to idly watch—I had to do something.
I searched the boathouse for some turn-of-the-century
device designed for saving piers. Nothing. Only the mute
accumulated junk of a hundred years witnessed my frantic
search.

Then, from under the workbench a patch of grimy red
plastic caught my eye: my greasy Homelite chainsaw, oiled,
gassed, ready to go. I hefted 'er up, flipped the toggle,
popped the choke, yanked the starting cord: the engine
roared, the exhaust poured out and engulfed the boathouse,
the whirling circle of shiny teeth gnashing at the air. Ready
for business.

I tramped out into the fury. Immediately, I was
drenched by rain and spray. For a moment I studied the pattern of the waves, sizing up my enemies, their rise and fall,
the thrusting of the platform under the pier. Standing on
the boardwalk clutching the lethal weapon, I felt like Wyatt
Earp at the O.K. Corral taking on the James brothers. The
biggest seas rolled in between washboards of smaller swells.
There would be a moment, if I timed it just right, when I
could drop down on the platform and saw away its jutting
piling. With luck, once the piling was gone, I would be able
to push the floundering platform away from the pier. The
footing would be tenuous, the platform slick and bucking.
If I got washed off, there would be no hope of surviving

such turbulent undertow, such chilling water. The queasy reality grew clear to me: I could easily die.

"*Crash!*" Another plank spun away in the wind. My terror changed to anger.

"*Crack!*" One more wave, another timber splintered.

The sea flattened down for an instant and the wind paused to catch its breath. No time to waste! With the chainsaw idling, I slid over the side of the pier onto the heaving raft.

From the northwest rolled the breakers, a field of frothing mountain ridges sweeping in on me. Seawater swirled around my legs, the platform lurched and wallowed. While watching for the next great wave, I raised the chainsaw and gunned the throttle. Vicious teeth ripped at the piling, but it seemed to cut so poorly: I'd neglected to sharpen the chain!

Suddenly, a behemoth wave bore down on me, its broad shoulders rumbling in, higher than the rest. Would it erupt under the platform and crush me against the pier? Or break on the ledges and wash me away? I forced the snarling saw as hard as I could, my hands white with fear, white with cold, white with the blood all gone, shut off by my clenching grip. Wood chips sprayed wildly in wind. Above me I felt the big sea rise, start to turn, gain speed and altitude. Only a heartbeat to go. A fraction of a breath. A millionth of a second.

Just in time, the saw cut through. I clambered wildly back onto the pier with the chainsaw still whining, while the big sea broke open, capsizing the raft in an explosion of water. Free of its piling top, it swept away from the pier, sucked into the channel by the undertow.

I squished into the boathouse with the saw still sputtering. The ruins of the old platform washed out to sea, splintered planks and battered logs destined to become driftwood, to be washed ashore on a faraway beach, bleached by sun and softened by time, a curiosity to be discovered by some unknown strolling beachcomber who will poke at the scarred remains and wonder where they came from, what purpose they had served.

The saw had done its job. I shut it off, retired it under the bench. Only then did I notice the tremor of my hands. My heart palpitated fiercely, too. I had been a fool. I could have been killed, a bloated corpse pickled in brine. Never again will I be so reckless. As I stood in the darkened boathouse, the rain still pelting through the door, Billy's words returned to haunt me.

"Hard place to keep a pier," he had said.

BERNADINE'S CORNED HAKE

3 pounds fresh hake
8 medium potatoes, pared
1 large onion, diced
1/4 pound salt pork, finely diced
salt

Sprinkle hake with salt and refrigerate overnight. Put pared potatoes in large kettle and add just enough cold water to cover them. Cook until half done. Add hake and cook until potatoes are fork-tender. In small skillet, fry pork slowly, conserving liquid fat. Serve hake and potatoes—let your dinner guests add the fixings the way they like: onions, fried pork and renderings, salt and pepper, maybe some additional vegetables, too (turnips, squash, tomatoes, whatever the store has on the shelf). Makes enough for a hardworking fishing family.

6

AN ISLAND ODYSSEY

Mid-January 1987

DURING OUR FIRST SUMMER HERE I thought my island was nirvana. But then the hard, icy winter arrived, endless months of it. The sun rose too late and set too soon. Whenever I skied into town to do my errands, the post office was empty (nobody to chat with) and the store shelves were bare (out of Reese's peanut butter cups). The harbor seemed abandoned. *Islander* was there, of course, and a few other fishing boats, but the summer flotilla had disappeared, migrated to safer ports or hauled ashore in Stonington for winter repairs. No one at Town Hall, either. No one at Billy's shop. Back to the lighthouse I schussed, the nor'west wind tearing at my face, hard and bitter and dry. It drove us all inside. Tempers got short. Walls closed in. Alcatraz.

To try to shake off my black mood, Judi and I decided to flee south with Matthew. Perhaps a tonic of tropic air and serene beaches would nurse me back to reality: we focused our trip on Disney World.

We landed in Orlando laden with cameras and tour books and summer shorts dug out of storage. The skies were sunny and warm, but the fog of gloom

had followed me. I groused about the crowds and the congested freeways. I complained about the waitresses and the
creep at the car-rental place. The air was too warm, the
concrete too hard, the sky too blue. What a pathetic city! It
smacked of poor planning and monotonous predictability,
tattooed everywhere with the corporate signatures of fast
food and big oil.

Our motel room reeked of disinfectant and stale ciga-
rette smoke. Laced with safety chains and sliding bolts, the
steel door sported peeping holes to watch out for bandits,
rapists, and ax-wielding psychopaths. I ranted about the
stupid bluebell pattern on the bathroom tile and the grisly
teal lamp shades, then groaned into a chair and glared at the
wall.

"Just wait 'til we get to Disney World, Dad," said Matt.
"In Disney World everything turns out cool."

I watched Judi's face sadden as she worked a brush
through her hair, watching me in the plastic-gilded mirror
bolted to the wall.

An hour later we entered the Magic Kingdom. I stood
stupefied by the medieval castles and jutting mountains,
turn-of-the-century villages, and trolleys through fairy
kingdoms. Fantasyland, Frontierland, Adventureland—all
the fantasies that fools hunger for, rising ridiculously from
the residue of Central Florida's drained swamps.

I glowered cynically. "I'll be a grump," I said to myself.
"They'll never humor me."

But while I moaned and griped, everyone else's fun
increased. How dare they play while I felt sad! Judi and
Matthew left me to stew, skipping off to ride a mining train
through the Dakota Hills.

I sulked alone through the maze of storybook settings,
muttering about "values," and "priorities," and "quality of
life." The sun beat down. My throat got dry. My head began

to pound. The cacophony of calliope music and laughter rose to a din, then everything began to swim before my eyes. The sideshows and attractions merged one into the other, creating a blur of comic book clutter, swarming with sweaty tourists and loud-mouthed brats with dripping ice cream cones. A million pairs of eyes—all of them staring at *me*.

"Morons!" I snarled to myself. "Don't you understand? You're the victims of illusions, hoaxes, and shams."

A mechanical parrot laughed at me from an overhead perch. Behind me, there was a taunting "Yuk, yuk, yuk" from a trophy-studded wall, where the head of a silly moose peered down, his glassy eyes watching me as I tried to elude his gaze. Processions of molded Disney characters closed in on me, swaying like tottering zombies, their eyes unblinking, their frozen fiberglass mouths agape with the lyrics of worn-out songs that blared from hidden speakers.

"It's a small world, after all . . ."

The melody seeped out of the pavement and wept from the roofs. The growing crowd surged toward me, hoards of Minnie Mouse groupies rampaging through the park like a prairie fire across the Serenghetti, engulfing every inch of blacktop.

"It's a small, small world, after all . . ."

I retreated to a nearby concession stand. From a black woman in a Heidi costume I bought an extra-large cola (maybe I'd swig down a dozen or two). Now all I needed was a place to collapse. On the edge of this labyrinth of madness, I found an empty bench, a corner where I could guzzle, a spot where I could hide and feel as bad as I wanted. I slurped my soda until the familiar fire of heartburn rose and the belching started.

Then, beyond the milling crowd, I saw something green. It rose above the careening joyrides and the facades of make-believe, a verdant sponge of softness caressing the

Florida sky. A mirage, probably. I looked again, squinting to
check my vision. Trees! Real trees, I was sure of it! I found
Judi and Matt and we pushed our way through the crowd,
me pulling them along, plunging toward the shade. We
arrived at the foot of a towering grove, and there before us
rose an amazing sight: the Swiss Family Robinson Tree
House Pavilion, built on a real deserted isle.

We got right in line.

Before us, gargantuan trees stretched toward the heavens. A curling staircase fashioned from hand-hewn planks
and old ship's rigging coaxed us into the trees. As we
climbed, curtains of lacy leaves draped around us. The coos
and hoots of unseen birds came from everywhere, and the
scent of the jungle was so sweet I wanted to lick the air.

Farther we climbed, new discoveries greeting us at
every turn. Evidence of shipwrecked settlers: tools and
buckets, water wheels, laundry to dry.

High in the treetops, we arrived at the Robinson cottage, an elfish abode crafted from weathered driftwood and
the flotsam of scuttled ships. Each of us took a turn to peek
through the tiny window and see what waited inside: wire-
rimmed reading glasses left on an open book, a partially
prepared meal, a familiar coat hanging by the door. Each
passing tourist fantasized about living there.

"Absolutely heavenly!" raved the bald man.

"It's so quaint!" squeaked the fat lady in the Niagara
Falls T-shirt.

"I would give anything to live on an island like this!"
crooned the little girl with braces and braided hair.

I, too, felt oddly attracted. Maybe I was disoriented by
the thinner atmosphere so far above the earth. Or maybe
some mind-altering contagion from these tree-creeping
folk had infected my senses. Or perhaps my resistance had
simply run out, my heart won over to Disney's appeal.

Whatever the reason, I had been converted, another gawking face in this infinite chain of pretenders.

Eager to caress this wondrous tree, I reached out to touch a bough. To my dismay, it was coarse and hard. I looked at the leaves more closely: plastic, of course! I scratched on the handrail I thought was wood: molded fiberglass! In my mind's eye the tree went into a whirling metamorphosis: it became a coldly commercial image on a drafting board, a phony fairyland forged from fire-belching blast furnaces and sprawling chemical plants. This was no tree—I'd been bamboozled by an impostor. There wasn't an organic cell in its bones. Nor in this fabricated "island" lump. Nor within the walls of this animated ghetto. Nor in the whole of metropolitan Orlando. Nor in the state of Florida, as far as I could see. The entire experience was sleight of hand, an illusion, a lie. And there was I: ol' nature boy, stumbling around in a fake concrete tree, peeking in windows with a million other voyeurs, each one getting off on the fantasy of living on a tiny remote isle.

Take me home to Maine!

I knew my frame of mind was out of joint, but I couldn't shake my nasty mood. Several days later we abandoned Orlando, me more cantankerous than ever, carping all the while about ill-mannered people and stinking air.

AT DUSK WE LANDED IN BOSTON. The terminal teemed with winter refugees: fresh tans from the Florida beaches, strawhats from Bermuda, flowered shirts from the Virgin Islands. Skiers too, from Aspen and Vail, wearing the latest in designer togs. Tired travelers sat waiting on crates of Florida citrus. Others napped in lobby chairs.

We found our gate: Bangor. With a sense of relief, we presented our boarding passes, lugged our stuff onto the

plane, and got an airline smile from the flight attendant
who waited inside.

As soon as I took that first look down the long tunnel
of faces, I was refreshed by what I saw; stocky men with full
beards, high-top boots, and baggy pants; round women
with knitting needles at work; adolescents with acne and
University of Maine sweatshirts bought big enough to last
more than a single year . . . all going home to Maine. It felt
so good to snuggle in amongst them.

East northeast, we climbed skyward. Below, urban glare
gave way to black space flecked with an occasional barn-
yard light or cut by the serpentine tracing of headlights
climbing a hill. We snoozed awhile. Then the plane fell
lower and the airport landing beacons rose to meet us, our
wheels grabbing hold of the runway with a thundering
squeal.

Snow. Beautiful, freshly fallen snow. Everywhere
mountains of it had been plowed back to make way for the
planes. The frigid air caressed me as we crunched across the
parking lot, and the crystal twinkle of winter lights was a
welcome greeting home.

We drove from the terminal, looped onto the highway
and over the bridge. The frozen river below shimmered
south, a broad arrow of ice rich with celestial glow, showing us the way back to Isle au Haut. Above us reigned a
clear sky, a carbon blanket glittering with a trillion pricks of
light. We wound along the country road from Bangor to
Bucksport, dipping, curling, bumping across railroad tracks,
our headlights illuminating the gabled ends of clapboard
farmhouses and the occasional sign of a local business—
Acadia Trap Mill, the Country Mouse Variety Store, Louie's
Second-Hand Haven, Bob's Small Engine Repair. We
stopped for gas at the Gateway Cafe. There, we lingered by
the river and watched the sky's wintry spectacle; it flick-

ered, it flowed, it blossomed pink and violet in a fiery display of northern lights.

The next morning we caught the sunrise mailboat. Home again, shipwrecked by choice on the island I love. My failed mission to cheer myself on Disney's fabled island made me aware of the treasure in my own life: the richness of clean air and winter silence, the wealth of empty trails and ruby sunsets, the bliss of Judi's Gooey Chocolaty Yummy Bars. And once I settled down to my winter routine of writing and cross-country skiing, I realized Disney World has its place too; why begrudge others their need to taste that life? In a wacky way, it reminds me of our idealistic years in Berkeley, of our unending search for the perfect community. Let's give Disney World a cheer for its global imagination, its delineation of good and evil. The Swiss Family Robinson Tree House Pavilion, the Keeper's House on Isle au Haut; these are only regeneration stations where folks can regain clarity about their goals in life, their mission, taking their inspiration from whatever guru they choose, whether a plastic mouse or a finback whale.

We all need an "island" somewhere. A private rooftop in Brooklyn may do, a favorite cafe in L.A., or a lone old oak in an Iowa cornfield. The sum total of all our little cubbyholes makes up the planet earth, and the earth is no more or no less than an atoll sanctuary itself, adrift in a vast sea of island stars that stretch forever.

GOOEY CHOCOLATY
YUMMY BARS

1/2 cup butter or margarine
1/2 cup sugar
1 1/2 tsp. vanilla, divided
1 cup flour
1/4 tsp. baking powder
1/2 tsp. salt, divided
1 cup brown sugar
2 eggs
1 cup finely chopped walnuts
1 cup semisweet chocolate chips

Cream butter, sugar, and 1/2 teaspoon of the vanilla until light and fluffy. In a separate bowl, combine flour, baking powder, and 1/4 teaspoon salt. Blend into creamed mixture. Spread into greased square baking pan. Bake at 350 degrees for 15 minutes. Remove from oven. Cool 5 minutes. Combine brown sugar, eggs, the remaining 1 teaspoon vanilla, and 1/4 teaspoon salt. Beat until thick. Stir in nuts and chocolate bits. Spoon over baked layer. Bake for 25 minutes at 350 degrees. Let cool and cut into 12 pieces. Perfect finish for a picnic lunch.

7

JUDI AND THE CHIEF

Early '60s, Summer 1987

LIVING AT A LIGHTHOUSE STATION may seem romantic, but for Judi our initial year on Isle au Haut and the frequent visits by the Coast Guard lighthouse tender were a disquieting reminder of her childhood on Cape Cod.

JUDI'S FATHER, CHIEF DONALD J. ORMSBY, was a silent man, paunchy and sad, who always fidgeted with his wedding ring and combed his straight hair flat across his head. In charge of the Cape Cod lighthouse in Truro, he ran a tight ship, browbeating the enlisted men and keeping the station spic and span. Through the week he was barracked there, while a few miles away, through the pitch pine forests and across the moor lands, his wife, Ida, and their five children lived in a little shingled house on the Pamet salt marsh.

When the Chief trudged home on weekends, he sat in stony seclusion in an overstuffed chair in front of the TV, watching the Red Sox and drinking beer. He was of no help to harried Ida, who split her time between dusting the shelves at the Truro Library and nurtur-

63

ing her kids. Although Ida believed in helping the children
in every way she could, the Chief always said they should
swim on their own.

Judi spent her summers splashing in the bay. On the
beaches and in the village, at Sunday mass and in
Schoonejongen's store, her infectious laugh and ready smile
made others feel alive, and her fiery long red hair and freckles brought sparkle to the town.

When winters came, the north wind howled across the
moors and the Pamet's tides rose and fell beneath a snowy
crust, leaving the little house surrounded by a tundra of
frozen cattails and buckled ice. Every morning, Judi
climbed aboard the yellow bus to Truro School, and came
home at dusk to snuggle by the hearth with little sister
Jenny and baby Weeshiebug, reading them library books
that Ida brought home.

Judi never learned much about the ocean. Hers was not
a fishing family, like her friends' in Provincetown. And none
of her kin worked the shipyards down the Cape, or the
charter vessels that took tourists out to Race Point to hand-
line for flounder. The sea, like the father who never taught
her its ways, remained a foreign thing.

AFTER GRADE SCHOOL, Judi went on to Provincetown
High and worked summers at the Dairy King on Route 6;
that's where I met her, on the Fourth of July weekend, 1961.

I was a summer kid from out of state, who arrived every
Memorial Day in a '56 Bel Air convertible with my record
collection and saxophone. During the days, I frolicked on
the beaches. At night, I washed dishes in the steamy kitchens
of Provincetown's restaurants; The Cottage, The Moors,
Peter's Hill Motel and Cocktail Lounge, The Ancient
Mariner, I worked them all. The world of clattering pots and

fry-o-lators captivated me. Homosexual cooks who boldly fried me free platters of fresh clams, sandaled beatnik waitresses who sneaked me half-finished beers, the ready walk-in freezers stocked with sorbet and steaks—this stimulating subculture and free-spirited town all made for easy living.

After the kitchens closed for the night, I hung around the nightclubs—I wasn't old enough to get inside. I'd slouch on the curb in front of the Atlantic House and soak up the sounds of Zoot Sims or Gerry Mulligan or Lambert, Hendrix, and Ross, their music pulsing through the shuttered windows and washing the narrow streets. On Sunday nights, I played Sousa marches with the Provincetown Community Band in the park behind Town Hall. And every afternoon before I went to work, I steered my Chevy into the Dairy King. Each visit found my sundae a little thicker with fudge.

I slept in my family's Truro cottage by the cold storage plant on the bayside. Late at night, I'd lie in my bunk and watch the oscillating beam from Cape Cod Light sweep over the moors. Even from two miles away, the brilliance kept me awake; the light spilled through the window, flushing my room with images of the red-haired girl at the Dairy King. Maybe she was awake too, watching the beam from her house, musing about the saxophone kid and eager to discover what waited on the other side of Cape Cod Canal.

For the next two summers, I picked up Judi every chance I had. I'd park the Chevy in the door yard and rap on the screen door. The Chief would be sitting there, retired now, a granite lump in the chair. "Yup," he'd grunt. A grudging approval for me to come in, a conversation and consent, a salutation and goodbye, all rolled into a single sound.

Judi and I wound the Chevy over every Truro road and explored all the alleyways of Provincetown. We would stop for a loaf of warm bread at the Portuguese Bakery, or at

Mary Spaghetti's for a bowl of kale soup. On Commercial
Street, we wandered though galleries and bookshops and
bought little bags of penny candy. On the bench in front of
Town Hall, we sat among the sidewalk artists, listened to
the rantings of beat poets at the Cafe Poyant, always joining in the late-evening parade through the streets: queens
and dykes, drunk fishermen spilling from the Fo'c'sle, artists
and bohemians, gawking tourists from Beach Point.

Then, from the outskirts of town, we would trek barefoot across the sea of naked moonlit dunes to one of the
empty outer beaches: Newcomb's Hollow, Pilgrim Springs,
Race Point, The Highest Dune. In the swales of willowy
grass, we would find a cubbyhole for shelter, where only
stars reflected in each other's eyes and our breathing was
matched by the thump of breakers and the swish of surf
sweeping sand. Then I'd take her home. Under the light left
on by the back porch we would linger and dream, until the
light flashed three times, the demand for her to go in, a
Coast Guard signal from a father who seldom spoke. Let
them swim on their own, he said.

In September of 1962, we gathered up our sleeping bags
and a few cardboard boxes of provisions, packing them all
into the Chevy's trunk; it was smoking badly by then, having never had an oil change. Ida bathed us in kisses and the
neighbors waved goodbye. In a cloud of smoke, we headed
off for New Orleans. Behind us, the Chief stood motionless
at the driveway's end, like an obscure civic statue, frozen forever in time.

JUDI AND I WATCHED the Coast Guard cutter *Bridle* steam
across Isle au Haut Bay toward us, a buoy tender following
in her wake. A few weeks earlier she had dropped anchor
in front of the lighthouse and Chief Hewitt had come

ashore to talk with us: the Coast Guard was going to reno-
vate the light tower. It would take all summer—repointing
the stone and brick, replacing the windows, the lens, the
batteries, installing a new photovoltaic panel, rebuilding the
sides of the walkway, constructing a new steel railing
around the lantern room.

Now, the two ships entered the Thorofare and cruised
slowly into Robinson Cove. *Bridle* waited while the tender
prodded the bottom with her electronic feelers. Men in
orange life vests scrambled about the decks. Radios bleated
back and forth. Finally, a heavy mooring was dropped and
the clattering clanking chains trailed after, tied off with a
red and white buoy where *Bridle* would lie for the summer.

For eight weeks Chief Hewitt's crew crawled over the
light tower. Suspended like spiders in a web of ropes and
bosun's chairs, they scraped away rust and old paint, replaced
crumbling mortar, and added new glass. The banister on
the spiral staircase received special attention: crusted with
countless coats of paint, it was stripped bare and carefully
dressed with five layers of varnish. By the end of the mission, the lighthouse would shine like new.

Over the summer I got to know the "Coasties" well.
Every morning they came ashore at our boat landing and
passed the back porch, always pausing to chat awhile. At the
end of the day, they trailed back down the path to the
boathouse and raced their skiff back to *Bridle*. Then, the
aroma of smoldering hickory and barbecue sauce would
creep across the water from the Weber grill they kept on
deck. In the evenings, the auxiliary engine ran, and electric
lights lit *Bridle*'s decks and filled her cabin windows.

One day Chief Hewitt invited us aboard. Judi declined.
She had no interest in the Coast Guard, she said. She stayed
ashore and took Thunder for a ride down the Western
Head Trail.

In midsummer I left the island to attend my twenty-fifth high school class reunion in Columbus. Before leaving, I made sure the propane bottles were full, the skiff was tied tight, the charge in SweetiePie's battery was up to snuff. Although I had developed a checklist to prepare for my absences, one never knows what might go wrong.

I left on the early mailboat. Buster spent the morning in Stonington, loading *Mink* with freight. At noon, he returned to the island. Ile and Tim helped Judi off-load our supplies, then left her bobbing on the float, surrounded by cases of Martinelli's sparkling cider, a tire repaired at Steve's Garage, bags of whole wheat flour, a square of cedar shingles for reroofing the porch, paint for the barn, linens from Eldridge Jobbing House, a long-awaited thermostat for SweetiePie, and two hundred pounds of oats for Thunder. It all had to be lugged up to the inn, a hundred yards away. Judi had to do it alone.

Unexpectedly, the young Coast Guardsmen rushed to our dock in the *Bridle's* skiff. They grabbed hold of the boxes and bags and hauled them up the hill, making a game of it and having fun. Soon the job was done. Judi put the kettle on and whipped up a batch of tangy lemon squares dusted with confectioner's sugar. The young men entertained our guests with stories of Coast Guard rescue missions while Heather served tea and goodies. Even Judi mingled awhile, pleased that the Coasties had been so helpful.

The next morning the generator started running wildly. With the generator out of whack, the water pumps won't run. If the pumps don't run, there's no water for the guests to shower, no water to flush the johns. Judi went down to the generator shack and started fooling with the control panel, poking at the wiring with a screwdriver. Out of nowhere, a blue-shirted arm reached over her shoulder and slammed closed the knife switch.

"Careful there!" shouted Chief Hewitt. "There's enough power in those circuits to boil your blood."

Judi jumped back. "I thought . . . maybe a loose wire or something," she stammered. Was it possible this military man, with his silly butchcut and badges, actually cared about her plight?

"I'll get Lee and Doaks," he said, turning on his heel.

Soon, two boyish engineers from *Bridle* arrived. Toolboxes clinked open, sleeves were rolled up, and within the hour the generator purred like new. Then the Coasties put away their tools and headed back to *Bridle*. Judi left too, winding back up the trail to the inn, a hint of a smile crossing her face. It was nice having the Coast Guard around. Maybe they weren't so bad after all.

After such a trying day, Judi needed some relaxation. Grace had arrived for a visit and Matthew had nothing to do, so the three of them decided to row up the Thorofare, pick up the mail, and gossip a while at the store.

They took neighbor Mitzi's Swampscot dory, a tippy flat-bottom boat. Matt lay in the bow, his arms hanging over the gunwales. Grace slumped in the stern. Judi rowed. Like three sardines in a can, they wallowed up the Thorofare. Aided by the prevailing breeze and the incoming tide, they worked their way up the channel past *Bridle*, past the fish weir, past the spindle where the osprey fed her chicks, past Bernadine, who leaned out her door and waved.

After completing their errands, they cast off from the Town Landing and started rowing back toward the lighthouse. As soon as they broke around the weir, they realized they should have turned back: the wind had picked up dramatically and the tide was running against them. But it was getting late, and there was dinner to cook and the needs of guests to tend. Maggie and Thunder would be hungry, too.

It took an hour of struggle before they reached the
cove. The Coasties had returned to *Bridle* and were celebrating the end of the workday. While Judi, Grace, and
Matthew wrestled with the oars, Springsteen howled from
the ship's stereo, and across the water wafted the aroma of
burgers sizzling on the barbecue.

Foot by foot, Judi battled across the cove. Here, the protection of the shore fans away, increasing the exposure to southwest seas. Fitful gusts hit the dory, throwing her off course.

Judi rowed heroically, but her tired arms couldn't control the heavy oars: they kept slipping from the locks and
slamming her knuckles.

Then, a sudden swell was upon them, its mass rising,
turning, folding, crashing against the bow. Matthew was
deluged in frigid water, his shirt soaked, the icy brine running down his back.

"Careful, Mom!" he shrieked, his thin white fingers
clenched on the gunwales. "Head for shore!"

"I'm afraid to," she cried. "Waves are too high; we'll roll
over in the trough."

With her back to the waves, Judi didn't see what was
coming next.

"Hang on, you guys!" screamed Grace, her terrified
eyes focused on a monster swell that rushed forward, building as it bore down.

Judi turned to look. Just as she shifted her weight, a
gust hit the dory, pushing it sideways. The tumbling swell
burst against the hull and slopped into the boat.

"DAMN!" cursed Judi.

"GOD!" howled Grace.

"MOM!" wailed Matthew, pleading for motherly reas-
surance.

Each breaking sea added more to the growing lake that
washed around their feet. Grace bailed furiously with a cut-

off Clorox bottle. Judi's arms ached and her bloody-knuckled hands were numb, but she kept hacking away with the oars. She looked over her shoulder to measure the distance to the boat landing; there, directly off the bow, loomed *Bridle*, like the Rock of Gibraltar.

Judi had visions of her father flash back, frozen in his living room chair. Already saved twice in a day, she hoped she could depend on this other Chief: would he come to her rescue again? Drenched and shaken, she pulled parallel to *Bridle*.

Out of the cloud of barbecue smoke, the six Coasties scuttled to the edge of the deck, lining up in a perfect row, as if for an officer's review; Judi shipped her oars. But no line was thrown to the dory, and *Bridle*'s skiff remained fast on its painter. Would they have to scream for help? Where was the Chief? Why didn't he come to the rescue? Then the line of boyish faces broke into impish grins (they thought the three were doing fine, having rowed all the way from the Town Landing): they saluted the trio in the half-sunk dory, and broke into joyous song:

> Row, row, row your boat
> Gently down the stream
> Merrily, merrily, merrily, merrily,
> Life is but a dream.

They sang it in rounds, each doublet joining in with military precision, six voices singing as sweetly as school children. It was a song that shattered Judi's hopes. Occupied somewhere below deck, the Chief never appeared.

For a moment, Judi sat paralyzed. She glanced at Grace, who shuddered in the stern, waiting to be lifted from the floundering dory. She looked at Matthew shivering in the bow, pleading for parental assurance. Then she sat up,

squared her shoulders, and seized the oars with a reserve of
power she never knew she possessed; the dory lunged forward with the oars pounding the water like hoofbeats. Her
face streaked with seawater, her freckles glittering like dia-
monds, her red mane rippling in the wind, she jockeyed the
little dory proudly across the cove. Judi had learned to swim
on her own.

IDA'S SEA CLAM PIE

1 double pie shell (see crust recipe for Judi's Perfect Apple
     Pie, following chapter 2)
10 to 12 sea clams (hen or surf clams), ground or chopped
     (save juice when opening clams)
1 large piece salt pork, sliced fine
1 medium onion, chopped
1/2 tsp. pepper
2 Tbs. butter
2 Tbs. lemon juice

Fry chopped onion in salt pork until tender. Remove salt pork. Add clams and 1/2 cup clam juice. Let simmer on low heat until tender, about 10 minutes. Sprinkle with pepper and lemon juice. Put mixture in pie shell. Add a small amount of juice. Reserve remaining juice for gravy. Pat butter on top of clams. Add top crust. Bake 10 minutes at 450 degrees and 30 minutes at 350 degrees. While pie is baking, prepare gravy.

GRAVY: Make a roux with 2 tablespoons of butter whisked into 2 tablespoons of flour. Add clam juice and allow to thicken over heat. Add a bit of milk.

Serve pie hot out of the oven topped with gravy.

THE BELL

8

July 1988

OLD PHOTOGRAPHS SHOWED the Isle au Haut fog bell suspended from a cantilevered beam on the seaward side of the lighthouse, forty feet above the clutching surf. But when we arrived in 1986 to take over the lighthouse station, only a faint scar of mortar and paint remained to show where the bell had been.

Esther Robinson, whose family moved here from Matinicus Rock eighty years ago, was the daughter of the first lighthouse keeper. She was ten years old when she helped her father light the lantern for its inauguration on Christmas Eve, 1907. She remembers watching him tend the bell whenever fog banks shouldered their way into the Thorofare. In the wispy glow of the light, he would descend the front steps and make his way across the boardwalk to the tower as the mist and soupy blackness swallowed him. For as long as the harbor was thick-a-fog, he would go back every six hours to wind the weights that kept the bell tolling. Helen Barter, the island's postmistress, also grew up at the lighthouse, her father serving as the second keeper until 1935, when the tower

was automated. But neither Esther nor Helen knew the fate
of the missing bell.

Nor did Aubrey Greenlaw or any of his family who
owned the station before us. None of the villagers could
recall what had become of it, either. In most cases, the dispo-
sition of optics and fog signals from our nation's lighthouses
is well recorded, either in keeper's logs or in records main-
tained by government agencies or in the National Archives.
But the old brass bell at Isle au Haut simply vanished.

Its whereabouts was always the subject of local conjec-
ture. One theory was advanced by Bones McDonnell, my
friend who helped me build the temporary landing platform. One afternoon we were painting the front porch and
stopped to admire the tower. I asked him if he had any idea
what had happened to the bell.

"Nor'wester," he said. "That's what took 'er."

"Sure," I mocked, "a storm with an extension ladder."

His eyebrows crooked and his lip gave a twitch, so
noticeable it wasn't hidden by his bushy mustache.

"Never underestimate the power of the sea," Bones
said. He paused to rub at a smear of paint on the back of
his hand. "That little blow that washed away your temporary dock—why, that was just a breath. You haven't been
through a real storm yet. We get a corker every year or two:
when those rogue winter seas build and the nor'west howls,
the mere creations of mortal men are always vulnerable."

I shut my mouth and listened.

"I've seen storms toss ten-ton blocks of granite as if
they were marshmallows," he said, gazing respectfully across
the placid water.

"So, you think a storm simply swept away the bell?" I
asked.

Bones dipped his sash brush in the can and drew it out,
dragging the bristles across the pail's lip to remove the

excess paint. "I've heard the fishermen say, " he said, a twinkle in his eye, "that following a wicked nor'wester, when
the seas run nasty and the water churns deep, sometimes
you can still hear the old bell reverberate as it rocks in its
salty grave."

DURING THE SUMMER THE INN THRIVED, time passed
quickly. In July, I took a day trip to the mainland to search
for a few additional chairs for our guest rooms. Driving
through Searsport, which boasts the title "Antique Capital
of Maine," I surveyed the used-furniture barns and the
antique shops that hunker along the sides of U.S. 1. When
an overloaded hay wagon strayed across the road, I had to
brake unexpectedly and veered sharply onto the shoulder.
There before me sprawled a giant flea market. Between the
banks of tables piled high with mounds of merchandise,
streams of people eddied, their suntanned faces and bright
T-shirts sparkling like moving current. Something about
the spirit of the place called out to me. I parked and
climbed out to investigate.

I strolled through the maze of junk and tables. The eco-
nomics of a flea market is something I've always admired:
it's the last enclave of free enterprise. Like an Arab bazaar,
participants in a "flea" personalize the market experience,
negotiating prices, socializing with neighbors, competitors,
and customers. I wish we could buy auto insurance like
that, and missile defense systems, too. But nowadays we
can't even grab a hamburger without being yammered at by
a faceless squawking electronic box.

On the far side of this sea of secondhand goods stood
a ramshackle woodframe building. Irresistibly, I was drawn
toward it. I floated through knots of shoppers and skirted
hot dog stands until I found its entrance. Its porch sagged

from the weight of wagon wheels and steamer trunks filled
with the worn possessions of forgotten mariners. Orange
crates and handmade boxes bulged with dull-edged ship-
builders planes and farmers tools from bygone eras.
Broken-down baby buggies were jammed in everywhere,
heaped with tangles of tarnished kitchen utensils, old bottles, kerosene lanterns. In and out of the entrance wandered
a procession of bargain-hunters, the door propped open
with a milk can painted with blazing roses and the inscrip-
tion "Home Is Where the Heart Is."

The irrepressible force that had led me here became
even more powerful, coaxing me up the rickety steps. I
stopped in the center of the porch, turned, looked over my
shoulder. I gasped and held my breath: by the side of the
building, bolted to a hitching post, stood an elegant old iron
bell, beautifully cast, serene in its patina of rust.

Instantly, I began to dream, to scheme, to conspire. All
it needed to restore it to its glory was a bit of wire brushing and a coat of charcoal paint, maybe a sturdy bracket to
support it on the front of the Keeper's House, with a length
of pot warp dangling down for a tolling cord. How far, I
wondered, would its chiming reverberate across the water?

But I had to move fast—who knows when someone
else might make a move on my bell? A sly plan was needed.
Maintaining a cool head and suave approach, first I scouted the premises. Next, I practiced being disinterested,
silently rehearsing my lines and developing my tactics, leaving no margin for error. I waited for my heartbeat to nor-
malize and for the trembling in my knees to slacken while
I practiced my story a final time. Then, with practiced non-
chalance, I ventured inside.

Musty and dark as a pack rat's hole, the interior was
even more congested than the porch. Century-old portraits
of family patriarchs peered from the rafters. Stacks of

crumbling *Life*s and *National Geographic*s threatened to avalanche from makeshift shelves. Impaled on the walls, a hideous collection of decaying stuffed animals gazed hungrily at the shoppers.

It was easy to spot the shopkeeper: he was centrally located, in the midst of all the bargain hunters. A cherubic fellow, he wore paisley Bermuda shorts and a Red Sox baseball cap. The vestige of a cigar protruded from his mouth, its smoking tip bobbing as he stood guard and hooted at the browsers who foraged through his shop.

"That's five bucks, lady. No, I can't let it go for three— how you expect me to pay my rent? Hey Mac, watch the 78s, they get all scratched, ya know. You got to take all three of them bottles, lady: they go as a set. You break 'em, you buy 'em!"

This wouldn't be easy.

First, I'd hit him with my ice-breaker.

"Nice day, ain't it," I said.

"No, it ain't," he blurted. "All day long you people rummage through the merchandise and never buy a thing. Complaints, that's all I ever get."

"Sorry," I said, feeling responsible for his misery. But then I caught myself: I figured his griping was just a ploy, a method of distraction to break my concentration and set me up.

His fingertips rat-a-tat-tatted on the cover of an old Victrola he used for a desktop. He just stood there, watching me, waiting. Timing was everything—I moved in for the kill.

"What do you have to get for that rusty old bell out there?" I casually asked.

His cobralike stare locked onto me. I was a hunk of pulsing meat, being stalked by an old-time trader who gauged his victims by the part in their hair, the scuffs on their boots.

His stubby fingers groped for the soggy cigar and dislodged
it from the cradle between his lips. Ash tumbled to earth.

"You a dealer?" he snapped.

"Who . . . *me?* No, I only wanted to . . ."

But I had reacted too quickly, his sudden interrogation
catching me off-guard, delivering a perfect *coup de grâce* to
my act, exposing my amateur tactics, my hollow bluff.

He knew he had me: he grinned, a wide, smug grin
that stretched from ear to ear and made his whiskers bristle. The cigar shifted slightly in the vise-like grip of his
teeth, his eyes never relaxing from their hypnotic hold. I
was helpless. In desperation, I threw myself at his mercy.

"Look, the truth is, I really like the bell," I said. "I want
it, but I can't afford much. Can you give me a break? How
about a swap? I'll UPS you a gallon of my wife's famous
curried chicken laced with oregano and almonds."

"No way, Sport. I got to have seventy bucks," he said
flatly, sucking on his stogie.

"How about sixty?" I countered.

"No chance!" he snorted. He turned his back and
started dealing out baseball cards on the Victrola top, sort-
ing them into divisions.

I felt humiliated. He was making me pay the price for
my meager offer. I'd do anything to correct my blunder.

Then, his fat fingers ceased their dealing. He looked
up. A smile spread across his whiskered face.

"Tell ya what, Bub. I'll make ya a deal. I'm sick and
tired of all these creeps pawing through my stock. They
treat my stuff like junk—at least you found something you
like! Make it sixty-five."

I couldn't chance the possibility of things going awry;
there would be someone else behind me, someone else
eager to grab the bell at any price, perhaps dozens more
waiting in the wings.

"It's a deal!" I rejoiced, reaching for my checkbook.

We made our way to the porch and he helped me unbolt my prize. Jubilantly, I lofted it to my shoulder, letting the smooth round edge of the bell spread the weight across the back of my neck. He stuffed my check into a shirt pocket. "Yep," he marveled, "you folks really go for them bells. And I only got eight left from my last shipment!"

It was about fifty yards to the truck, and I figured my shoulder could endure the bell's piercing weight just long enough for me to cross the parking lot. As I staggered through the labyrinth of plywood tables, I suddenly became aware of people watching me.

"Look, Stanley," I heard one woman call to her husband. "That man—he bought the bell!"

Another bystander, a short wiry fellow with a Maine Black Bears T-shirt, rushed over and grabbed me by the elbow.

"Good for you, Sonny," he said gleefully, slapping me on the back. "Good luck with the bell!"

Everywhere, people stared at me, pointing, smiling, and chattering excitedly. With my new acquisition seat-belted beside me, I drove off bewildered.

What is it about bells? Why do people find them so enthralling? Are they imbued with some universal appeal, some timeless function? They peal from the peaks of churches and schoolhouses. At one time, trains had them, ships and firetrucks too—as well as lighthouses. In an age where our ears are assailed by sirens, gunshots, and screams, the incessant drone of highways, traffic, the blare of boom boxes, and the garrulous profanity of celebrities and politicians, perhaps the bell's clear ring echoes the voice of a more tranquil time. We long for the basic and pure: the clang of iron against iron, the primordial call to convene, to lend a helping hand.

Today, my bell hangs from a beam on the front porch of the Keeper's House, freshly blackened, a tolling cord draped within easy reach. I use it to call my guests to dinner. I ring it to celebrate the birth of a child, to mourn the passing of a loved one, to welcome the dawn and to salute the setting sun. Of course, it marks the completion of my renovation of the lighthouse station, too. But most gratifying of all, during those summer evenings when thick-a-fog rolls across the Thorofare, I stand on my front porch and faithfully toll the bell. The clarity of iron ringing through the mist—that's a welcome signal to any wandering soul seeking anchorage for a night.

CURRIED CHICKEN WITH
ALMONDS

4 whole chicken breasts, split
1 tsp. paprika
1 tsp. celery salt
1 tsp. oregano
1 1/2 tsp. curry powder
1/2 tsp. pepper
1/4 cup melted butter
1 cup sliced almonds
1 pint sour cream

Combine seasonings, stir into butter. Place chicken in baking dishes and pour seasoning mixture on top. Bake at 350 degrees for 30 minutes. Spread sour cream over chicken. Top with almonds. Bake 30 minutes more. Serves 8—a zesty warm meal for a cold, foggy night.

9

FOGBOUND

August 5, 1988

DAWN. ANOTHER FOGGY DAY. Was it seven in a row? Or eight?

The first to rise, I wandered through the pea soup with my saxophone. I found myself on the boardwalk to the light tower. Beneath me, the planks arched like a bridge through clouds. A vapory spruce tree, a wispy ledge of stone, my faded house of sleeping people: all around me, the once-familiar landmarks of my front yard emerged and dissolved in mist, irresolute ghosts unsure of where they belong.

I adjusted my neck strap and fingered the keys. Should I rouse my guests with "Misty"?

During our first two years here, I had played at 7:15 every morning in the foyer. It was different back then—we rented only three rooms, and the guests were always asleep at that hour.

It worked like this: In the living room I'd quietly assemble the old tin horn my mother gave me in junior high, and sidle soundlessly to the bottom of the stairs. Wetting the reed with saliva, I'd listen for the telltale sound of

any waking guest. Assured that all were still asleep, I'd fill
my lungs with the ocean air that flowed in through the
screen door, close my eyes, feel the coolness of the ivory
keys beneath my fingertips, let my mind empty, my soul
ruminate. Then, I'd focus on the dog-eared scores clamped
in my lyre. When I started on the first piece only a faint hiss
of air escaped between my reed and mouthpiece. Then, the
first few notes slipped free, so delicate and far away that
even the mice sleeping in the pantry wall were unaware I
played. As my volume increased and the tempo quickened,
my offerings curled up the stairwell, seeped under bedroom
doors, tiptoed across feather pillows, eased between warm
sheets, joining dozing lovers with invasions of their beds.
One by one, they began to open their eyes. Groggy minds
began to recall where they were, here between these pastel
walls and windows filled with sea and light. And only then,
as they became fully awakened, did the slurred crescendos
and amblings of eighth and quarter notes coalesce into
songs they recognized: "Morning Has Broken," "Bridge
over Troubled Water," "Stormy Weather." Then, from my
station at the bottom of the stairs I'd hear a mumble or two,
the squeak of a bedspring, the thump of feet crossing the
floor. A latch would click open. Filling the crack in the
door, the toe of a slipper and a curious sleepy eye searched
for the source of the music. But by then, I would be gone.

That's the way it used to be, before we added three
more rooms. Now, there are too many people. Invariably, an
early-rising bird-watcher or an exuberant jogger comes
skipping down the stairs before I have a chance to play—
like Mrs. Clukey, who, on this particular morning, peered
from her bedroom window into the fog searching for me
(she was always up by five). I didn't want to play for her. I
never perform well in front of live audiences, and I'll tell
you the reasons why.

As a high school senior, I performed Claude Debussy's "Snowfall" before the assembled student body. Halfway through, my F-sharp key stuck and the rest of the piece was wracked with screeches. I was mortified. And when I auditioned for the second alto chair in a city-wide jazz band, my neat little regurgitations of memorized passages wilted lifelessly when challenged by the wailings of a beret-wearing freshman from Central High. I was tone-deaf. I had no rhythm. I couldn't play by ear. As an adult, I have limited my musical participation to occasional stints in small-town bands, performing in Fourth of July parades and convalescent homes. I toot with senior citizens and pimply-faced kids, the Tupperware lady with the glockenspiel and the mustachioed clerk from the hardware store who blasts the slide trombone. We hack through medleys of old Broadway tunes, bleat out R. B. Hall's "Independencia," and chase wildly out of control through "Stars and Stripes Forever." I'm forever shuffling through sheet music searching for the proper score, while all around me the band plays on. So, the sight of any early-rising guest like Mrs. Clukey made me sneak away with my saxophone. I preferred the anonymity of playing while everyone slumbered.

I moved around the side of the house to escape, retreated to the mudroom, and stashed my sax. I was grumpy and frustrated already. Maybe it was the lousy fog, so many days of it—and the musical requests that never ended. Recently, the *New York Times* had printed a nice article about the Keeper's House. I'm not one to look a gift horse in the mouth, but why did they have to say that I serenade everyone with my saxophone? With my leaden fingers and hokey repertoire, I knew I was disappointing.

Throughout the day the gloomy air thickened even more. Too much fog always causes problems. Mr. Dombrowner, our guest in the Garret Room, got lost at

Seal Trap. He had gone there with his crab salad sandwich
and an old volume of Lawrence Ferlinghetti selected from
the parlor bookshelf. He followed the shore, then turned
inland to scale the cliffs. Somewhere, he got turned around,
slipped on a mossy root, and skidded down the hillside,
gouging his butt and losing my Ferlinghetti. We had a
search party ready to go when he finally came staggering
back.

The mailboat arrived. Buster had the radar and Loran
whirling, the VHFs crackling, the foghorn groaning. Strung
across the cabin, the running lights glittered like Christmas
decorations on a snowy winter night. Several new guests
straggled ashore, shaken and pale from the passage through
the vaporous labyrinth of ledges. One wobbly-kneed
woman clutched at my arm as I led her to the inn.

"What time do you play in the morning?" she asked. "I
don't want to miss a note."

What a relief it was to get them all into the dining
room! Judi and Heather had everything ready: a feast of
tangy broccoli soup, tabouli and chewy sourdough bread,
paprika-frosted Crab Imperial with homemade pasta, tender asparagus tips, and for dessert, gooey apricot torte.
While Heather served, I sorted recyclables and brought
cider from the cellar. Then I stoked a small fire in the parlor stove: the damp, cold weather would coax guests to
warm a bit before retiring for the night.

I leaned against the old Servel refrigerator and waited
to see what scraps would be left for my dinner. One of the
new arrivals, a fellow named Judd, breezed in to fetch his
Mondavi white. He looked at me and winked. "I read we
can expect a dazzling wake-up call," he said.

I could only mutter. The miserable weather was making me testy. Guests who ordinarily would evoke friendly
feelings only made me cross. I gave them forced smiles,

recited answers to the questions each new visitor inevitably
asks, tried in vain to match their bubbly vacation moods
when mine was as damp and heavy as the weather. Now,
my attempts at hospitality began to suffocate me. I couldn't
stand any more! Fortunately, when I turned to flee I found
an old friend waiting for me: from the corner of the mudroom, half buried beneath a mound of dirty dishrags and
foul-weather gear, beckoned my saxophone. Should I hang
around this stuffy kitchen only to uncork a few bottles of
wine? To answer silly questions? To carry out garbage and
gnaw on the charred remnants in the bottoms of scorched
pots? The hell with it all! I grabbed the sax and stalked out
the door.

Blackness. No stars overhead, no shapes beyond the
door yard. I descended the steps into the pale. Behind me,
the kitchen window wilted, with the night shift passing
back and forth across the fading square of light like mari-
onettes bobbing across a puppet stage. My face, hot and
sticky with the residue of the steamy kitchen, welcomed
the cool freshness. The solitude of the fogbound night—
that's what I was after.

With flashlight and measured footsteps I found the
boathouse door. A match brought to life the kerosene
lantern kept hung above the workbench. As I turned up the
wick, the light spread through the boathouse, exposing dark
corners and illuminating familiar forms reposed in the
shadows: ladders, barrels, lobster traps, my old vinyl chair by
the seaward door, and forlorn *Alma*, turned upside-down
on sawhorses, where she waits eternally for her bottom to
be caulked.

Hiding out in the fog. The opaque vapors surrounded
my boathouse barrow, apparitions drifting through the
door, the white shrouds reminding me of my ghostly
grandmother, her lacy smocks, her pale mouth, her frosty

kisses. I was alone with my feelings, my failures and fears, my dreams and passions, too, but when I closed my eyes and inhaled the mist, it felt good inside. Safe, here in the folds of the fog, there was nobody to snicker at my saxophone playing.

My thumbs found the catches of the familiar case. I raised the lid. The horn I'd known for forty years lay there in its worn purple velvet bed, a battered artifact, tarnished and chipped with the plating mostly gone, only patches of golden enamel here and there to reflect the lantern glow. Nicks, scratches, stains, and dents riddle the horn, each a reminder of glorious halftime shows, or a jam session in Jimmy Moynihan's barn, or clowning around in Bernadine's talent show. The cork crumbles from the neck, and the ancient key pads suffer from dryness and cracks. To make up for broken springs, an improvised system of rubber bands and paper clips fights off the wheeze of leaking air.

The moistness of the fog nurtured me: my fingers began to tingle and my mouth to salivate. Within me, a great confidence surged, a freedom to cut loose I never experienced while playing for fully conscious people. My eyes pressed closed and the mouthpiece found its place, plugging in, connecting to my gut. My tongue wetted the reed, my embouchure tightened. Then, unrehearsed tunes started to bleed from my lungs.

At first, the fog coaxed me to offer cautious tunes that flowed *molto lento*, strains from children's songs with images from Mother Goose, staccato rat-a-tat-tats from the drums of little tin soldiers, the lilt of a waltz for ballerinas and winged horses swaying in three-quarter time. But, little by little, my breathing quickened and my heartbeat soared and my gushings got more funky, and beneath my fingertips the pearly keys began to shudder, fed by nerve endings that pulsed from my heart, my pelvis, and my belly.

From deep inside welled musical extrusions I'd never let out before. Some were sorrowful weepings, mourning with flats and bendings. Others, *molto animato*, with spiraling strings of sixteenths that fluttered into the rafters. Each bleeding phrase was followed by a more impassioned one, while all around me the fog crowded in, coaxing me, feeding me, teasing me, caressing me, rooting me on.

My lungs pumped wildly with her vapors, sucking them in, transforming them to musical geysers that spewed from the bell of my horn, an eruption of never-spoken fantasies that have no place on earth—and the more I played, the more she craved.

Soon, my bellows and moans seeped through gaps in the window sash, bubbled from beneath the shingles, penetrated beyond the boathouse doors. Intertwined with the shimmering vapors, my outpourings danced across the water and trembled beneath the hidden moon. Racing couplets and triplets, caressed by semiquavers, built in a feverish crescendo to skyrocket over the bay. Fortissimo! Fortissimoooooo! Fortissimooooooooooooooo! . . .

Then, my diminuendos and codas brought me back to earth. An occasional grace note floated down. Like dying embers, my closing phrases faded into mist. Finally . . . only silence.

My body ached with happiness. I loved the fog—I had found an audience that didn't flinch at flat notes. She had been the inspiration for my saxophone and me, our energy, our lover, and now we felt so blissful, just the three of us. It seemed a little foolish, but others needn't know. The Dombrowners, the Clukeys, Judi and the kitchen staff, they would be gathered in the parlor for some after-supper chatter. The stove would need another log, so I disassembled my old tin friend and tucked her into the case. Then I lowered the lantern, blew out the flame, and left the boathouse,

plowing back into the blackness with my swaddled saxophone.

The night remained cold and wet. But as I wound
through the woods to the house, I felt above me a gasp of
light: overhead, a patch of clear sky had appeared, exposing
a clutch of burning stars. The opening grew, the fog curling
away within it. Perhaps my impassioned puffing had burned
a hole in the soupy ceiling, starting some celestial osmosis
that sucked away the vapors; who knows what misty mira-
cles might be accomplished with a magic horn. So, ever
since that joyous encounter I keep my saxophone clear of
clutter, the pads well greased, the keys well oiled. I even
replaced the old rubber bands with snappy new ones: the
next time I'm fogbound, I want to be ready.

CRAB IMPERIAL

1 pound crabmeat
1/2 cup milk
1 1/2 tsp. butter
1 Tbs. flour
1 egg yolk
1 1/2 tsp. lemon juice
1/2 tsp. Worcestershire
1 Tbs. mayonnaise
1/2 tsp. dry mustard
1/8 tsp. cayenne
1/4 tsp. white pepper
1/4 tsp. salt
1/4 tsp. pepper
paprika

Heat milk to boiling point. In skillet, melt butter and whisk in flour. Add milk, whisking until smooth. Add egg yolk, Worcestershire sauce, mayonnaise, and seasonings. Blend well. Gently add crabmeat. Spoon mixture into small buttered dishes.

Make a topping by melting 1/2 stick butter in skillet, adding 3 cloves crushed garlic. Fry. Add 1 1/2 cups bread crumbs, 2 teaspoons lemon juice, and 1/2 teaspoon pepper. Cover crabmeat mixture with topping. Sprinkle with paprika. Bake 15 minutes at 350 degrees. Makes 4 nice servings: it's rich and tangy, so the servings should not be too large.

10

COOLING WITH FLAMES

May 2, 1989

BUSY MR. DIGBY FROM MELROSE, MASSACHUSETTS, appeared in the kitchen doorway. He had left his cellular phone in the Horizon Room with his attaché case, its contents spread across his bed in a patchwork of files and reports.

"More coffee, please," he said to Judi. "I need it bad— I've got a lot of work to do."

He slopped his cup full with the Ethiopian-Colombian blend Judi keeps hot in a thermos, then slurped while he paused from his hectic schedule to marvel at Judi's domain. He watched her crank slabs of flattened dough through her pasta cutter and hang the noodles on the drying rack, the squeaks of the machine resonating in our spartan kitchen. His gaze moved around the room. He studied the painted pantry and the wooden countertops, the jars of sprouts that glistened on the window sill, the hanging pots of cilantro with aromatic leaves quivering in the ocean breeze. The simple room seemed to soothe this harried businessman from the high-tech world. He began to confide in Judi, telling her how peaceful he found it here, distanced from the electronic squalor of office life. But when he noticed the

Servel refrigerator standing in the corner, he became visibly dismayed. "Hey, what's with the fridge?" he complained. "I thought there was no electricity here."

"Jeffrey," she called to me. "Come talk to Mr. Digby. He wants you to explain the refrigerator thing."

I LOVE MY OLD SERVEL. The enamel may be faded and chipped, but even after sixty years, it keeps on working fine. With its smooth curving lines and old-fashioned door, it looks just right in the lighthouse kitchen, and the friendly gush of its gas burner keeps me company when I'm here alone.

Mr. D. isn't the only curious one. Guests frequently quiz me about it, perplexed by how it runs without electricity, how it cools by burning gas. I was mystified myself, until a few years ago when I went to Bangor searching for a replacement door seal for it.

I LOCATED A RICKETY OLD STOREFRONT appliance shop on Main Street. It was a cramped place, congested with burned-out motors and pumps waiting for repair, ceiling-high shelves creaking with bins of valves and bolts. Every inch of floor space was crowded with secondhand washers, dryers, refrigerators, and stoves.

Behind the parts counter was an old fellow with thick eyeglasses and hanks of gray hair splaying out from under his engineer's cap. Thumbing through a bank of catalogs, he looked at me over the top of his spectacles and smiled when I inquired about the door seal. He tottered into the storeroom, skidded crates about with a pallet jack, and squeezed between legions of old washers dishonored with grime and dust. With a broom handle, he poked at a sag-

ging cardboard box on the highest shelf; it tumbled onto
the floor and a roll of rubber gasket sprang out around my
feet. He hacked off a ten-foot section and curled it like a
gopher snake into a paper bag.

"So, you got an old Servel," he said, his eyes glinting with
nostalgia. "She got a vertical burner, or a horizontal one?"

"Vertical," I said.

"Ah, yes. Them's the good ones," he said. "Harder to
keep the burner clean, but not as temperamental. The late
forties models—they're the best of all."

I asked him how they work. His whiskered face bright-
ened with enthusiasm (he was flattered that some layman
shared enough interest to ask). Turning over a sales sheet
and pressing it flat on the counter, he drew a pencil stub
from his shirt pocket and proceeded to sketch a diagram.

"Here above the burner sits a chamber filled with
ammonia and water," he began. "Just like a teapot, really,
except the rig is soldered up tight, so no gas escapes. As it
heats, the ammonia turns to vapor and rises up a pipe to the
condenser." He worked patiently with the pencil, using
arrows to show the path of the vapor.

"Couldn't it suddenly explode?" I blurted. "You know,
with all that force contained inside—like a plugged-up
pressure cooker?"

"No chance, son. You see, soon as the vapor rises it fills
this condenser up here on the top of the fridge. The condenser is a container all prickly with little external fins, lots
of square inches of metal to diffuse the vapor's heat. Well,
the vapor cools inside the condenser and turns to liquid
ammonia. Then it flows through these here tubes bundled
around the freezer compartment like pig intestines." He
squiggled a mass of loops around his crude drawing of the
freezer department to get across his point. "Here's the most
important thing to grasp: *pure liquid ammonia boils at 25*

degrees below zero. Imagine that! When something boils, it's using up energy (heat). So, as long as the atmosphere around the cooling tubes is above 25 degrees below zero, heat is transferred out of the air, literally sucked into the bowels of the cooling system. Lastly, the heat-laden ammonia runs back downhill, combining again with water, releasing the heat, and returning to the chamber over the burner."

The old man used the pencil stub to jab an emphatic period at the end of his explanations.

"Sort of a perpetual motion machine," I said, proud I'd followed his explanation.

"Yep, 'cept these ol' gals got no motors or moving parts: it's an old-fashioned apparatus that still makes sense," he said. "The entire cycle operates solely by gravity. And ammonia produces no chlorofluorocarbons, the ozone-depleting gas you get as a byproduct of freon—the stuff they use in modern refrigerators. And these old jobs are a sight more economical too, and downright logical. There's nothing to break or replace."

"Sounds like one way to preserve our environment," I chimed in. "Just think: if everyone used them, maybe we could slow down global warming. Do you sell new models here?"

"Nope," he said. "Haven't had 'em for years. Nobody else has, either; the company went out of business."

I HAVE TO TELL YOU THE TRUTH, HOWEVER: these old Servels are far from perfect. There've been times when mine's acted up. One morning, for no apparent reason, it started grumbling and hissing and belching rancid smoke. Bobby Turner heard we were having trouble and showed up. He is the island's wizard of old ways: he seduces extra miles out of abandoned trucks and finds leaks in roofs that others have given up on. He frequently appears out of the fog at just the

right moment, the pockets of his coveralls sagging with
screwdrivers and wrenches.

Bobby pried off the kick panel and we flopped on the
floor, stretching out on our bellies to explore the dark
world beneath the fridge: spider webs, dust balls, lost soup
spoons, bottle caps, lobster pegs, paper clips, and little clots
of dried-up gook. With a flashlight and a pair of pliers, he
probed and poked, examining her innards. He tugged on
tubes, jiggled valves, and checked for loose screws. Then he
hauled out the burner, scraped it clean with his jackknife,
and blew away the dust. Finally, he showed me how to
adjust the flame by twisting the little brass ring under the
burn tube.

"A steady, clear-blue flame," he said. "That's what we
want. With an inner core that just kisses the generator." He
remounted the burner, fiddled with the adjustment, and
tightened the bolt with a grunt. "Don't let 'er burn yellow
or white. Those flickering flames waste fuel and dirty up
your paint."

Perfectly tuned, the Servel's voice returned to an even,
mellow gush. We got to our feet and snapped the bottom
cover in place. Bobby wiped his hands on his coveralls; I
poured coffee.

"In the autumn, when you shut her down," he said,
"wedge an old Bicycle playing card over the burner,
cupped so it sheds any dust and carbon that crumble down
the stack. Keeps the air ducts from getting plugged. Then
every spring she'll fire right up."

While we sipped coffee and munched on slices of sour
cream coffee cake Heather brought back from the dining
room, I jotted down every bit of information Bobby
offered. With pounds of fragile Brie inside and lots of eggs
and fish, a breakdown could be disastrous in the middle of
the summer.

"As a last resort," said Bobby, tipping back his head to drain his coffee cup, "if you can't get it burning clean by adjusting the burner, roll 'er over on 'er top and leave 'er upside down overnight. Maybe give 'er a swat or two with a shaving strap. Sometimes that works—gives all the gas and liquids a chance to ooze back to where they belong."

OVER THE YEARS I'VE LEARNED to live with the idiosyncrasies of my old Servel. I've gained respect for its no-nonsense engineering, its durability and classic lines. It's evolved to perfection, like the cockroach, the snapping turtle, the rolling pin.

Then, one day last summer, I took the outboard down to the Town Landing to collect my mail. My post office box was stuffed. I clawed out the commonplace bills, the snaggle of brochure requests, a sale announcement from Dorsey's Furniture Barn, and a variety of weekly magazines and newspapers from the outside world, all the usual stuff that clogs my tiny box. But one piece caught my eye: a catalog specializing in technology for those who live off the beaten track. It featured solar systems, incinerating toilets, that sort of stuff. Seemed like a good source of equipment for the lighthouse, I thought, thumbing through the pages. Suddenly, in the center of the catalog this boldfaced announcement seemed to leap out at me:

$100 OFFERED TOWARD THE DISPOSAL
COSTS OF ANY SERVEL REFRIGERATOR

Advertising copy accompanying the offer made frightening claims that the Servels are safety hazards. Apparently, an elderly couple somewhere in the north woods had slept next to their Servel when the fridge had been badly out of

adjustment. Confined in their tiny camp, they had become
ill from carbon monoxide poisoning. But with hundreds of
thousands of Servels peppering the nation's backwoods and
mountains, it was a rare case of something going wrong. Of
course the catalog boasted an appropriate replacement, a
new high-tech model imported from Brazil, sleek and
shiny, designed to match the decor of your Winnebago or
ski chalet. It featured lots of extraneous gizmos and gadgets
to go with its flimsy doors, including a Teflon ice scraper, a
butter dish, and an internal light bulb that runs on batteries (not included). It cost a fortune, too.

No thanks—I'll stick with my old Servel. It was built
in accordance with an ethos that things should last, not fall
apart from shoddy craftsmanship and materials designed to
fail. Our world's resources, our fragile environment, our
water, air, and earth, are being harvested, mined, macerated,
boiled, broiled, and baked into a congealed toxic wasteland
of electroplastic junk, mass destruction weapons, sexist
Barbie dolls, astroturf, asphalt, and filth. The profit-makers
scream, "GROWTH." *But maybe profits and growth are the
problem!* Maybe we should shrink instead. Let's learn to
conserve and cherish and protect, to live more modestly.
Work less. Share jobs. Plant a garden. Bury the TV. Write a
book. Lend a neighbor a helping hand.

And let's rally around the heroes of sustainability who
can lead us toward a healthy future, like my persecuted gas
refrigerator. What a fitting sanctuary for it this island is!
After all, we're all renegades here, a congregation of beings
too enduring for the throwaway world. The reward offered
in that catalog was nothing but a scheme to ferret out these
surviving Servels, a bounty in fact, a price on the heads of
fugitive fridges that stubbornly refuse to surrender to the
consumer/profit gang. Like guerrilla chieftains waiting to
lead the charge, they still hide out in fishing camps, moun-

tain lodges, and island retreats, cooling with their little blue
flames. I'll continue to harbor mine, nursing its wounds and
feeding it gas. It deserves to live forever.

SOUR CREAM COFFEE CAKE

TOPPING:
1/2 cup chopped walnuts or pecans
1/4 cup sugar
1 Tbs. cinnamon

BATTER:
1/2 cup butter
1 cup sugar
1 tsp. vanilla
2 eggs
1 cup sour cream
1 1/2 cups unsifted flour
1 1/2 tsp. baking powder
1 tsp. baking soda
1/8 tsp. salt

Mix topping ingredients and put aside. Cream butter with sugar and
vanilla. Add eggs and sour cream. Combine dry ingredients. Add to butter mixture. Butter tube pan. Add half of mixture. Sprinkle with half of
topping. Add remaining mixture and sprinkle with remaining topping.
Bake 45 minutes at 350 degrees. Let cool slightly and cut in wedges.
Serves 8 to 10.

11

CASUALTIES

I NEVER THOUGHT A DINNER COULD END so disastrously. It had started in the usual way: guests mingling, exchanging names, sipping Chablis on the light tower boardwalk, the sun spreading its thinning coals across the watery horizon. At precisely 6:45, I climbed the front porch steps and hauled down on the bell cord. From along the shore my guests picked their way toward the dining room. I followed them inside. Behind me, the last slash of red sky sank behind the Camden Hills.

Each time Heather served a course, the sighs of contentment increased, an indication of satisfied palates and growing camaraderie. While I scraped at muffin tins in the kitchen sink, I chatted with our second chef, Lisa, who was cooking that night (Judi had taken Matthew off-island to shop for school clothes). Lisa, Heather, and I felt pleased with the way things were going: another houseful of sanguine guests, another successful meal.

After Heather presented dessert (tangy purple plum torte and freshly perked Sumatran coffee), I wandered through the hallway, lighting kerosene

101

lanterns, straightening bookshelves, while I listened in on the guests' conversation. The dining room candles were half-burned by then, the glow illuminating the circle of gathered faces like Sistine angels bathed in heavenly light. They laughed, told stories, spoke of trips to exotic destinations, revealed their worldly aspirations, their mortal fears, their victories, their pains and joys. At the appropriate moment, I drifted in with coffee cup in hand, as though it were unplanned. One fellow sprang to his feet and brought an extra chair from the living room to accommodate me at the table.

The conversation had turned to occupations. One young couple were bird-watchers from New York City who had come to watch the sharp-shinned hawks gather on Duck Harbor Mountain for the fall migration. Both worked as editors for major publishers. Another couple, in their fifties, hailed from a small midwestern town that boasted a noted liberal arts college. They taught in the philosophy department. For enjoyment, he played tuba in a polka band; she cultivated roses. On the far side of the table sat a frosty-haired beautician from Boston and her vacationing daughter, on leave from her stewardess job with Continental Airlines. They had come to simply spend time together.

Attention turned to the fourth couple, Dusty and Ann. I could feel the curiosity build, the American need-to-know-your-occupation-in-order-to-know-you syndrome at work. Dusty and Ann had come from Southern California to vacation in Maine, to "get centered," she had explained. Dusty was a stocky, unsmiling fellow with short-cropped blond hair, about forty-five, who participated little in the conversation. He had pushed his chair back from all the others, where the circle of candlelight barely found him. From there in the shadows, his eyes pierced the darkness like a cat's, scanning the table as though he were evaluating us, sizing us up, figuring his odds.

It was the youngest of the men, the editor, who finally asked the question. "And Dusty, what do you do?"

"I invent ways to kill people," he said.

Silence.

No one said, "Really?"

No one asked, "Why?"

No one asked where or how or when.

Only silence.

Clearing his throat, Dusty shifted his body and scooted his chair forward to enter the circle of light, claiming a place at the head of the table. His disconcerting announcement and abrupt emergence into the discussion cast a pall of intimidation over the dining room.

"I freelance for a major weapons designer," he said. "They let me develop whatever I want: booby traps, assassination devices, depopulation concepts, the works. I'm good at it. I earn top dollar. I do my job and I mind my business."

There was a muffled "Oh" somewhere from the other side of the table.

More silence. Napkins were folded and refolded. The beautician studied her fingernails.

Finally, the tuba tooter/professor spoke. "It's apparent that we have to educate the masses that these bloody wars are immoral. Interventions, that's all they are. Economic conquests. Noam Chomsky, in his recent essays on imperialism, points out that . . ."

"War is a fact of life," Dusty snapped. His eyes afire, he took the professor's opinion as a challenge to fight. "We gotta take a stand," he said. "If we don't protect ourselves by every means possible, the rabble will soon rule the world." He paused and glanced around the table at our bewildered faces, measuring the impact of his words. Smirking, he continued coldly, "This is a planet of contention, conflict, greed. Folks like you and me, we understand democracy and freedom, but the chaff of the world are lazy cannibals ready to devour everything we've built. We, my friends, must fight for our race."

Ann sat nervously, twisting her wedding ring.

I couldn't believe my ears. My sacred retreat was being violated, convoluted into a weekend getaway for a proselytizing Nazi. His presence here was a travesty of everything I stood for and made a mockery of the Keeper's House. But my professional role as innkeeper kept me from taking a stand, and the others remained as silent as I. Power, an ominous power, that's what Dusty conveyed, a power so sinister and profound that we all shrank from his challenge. He beamed with authority: he knew he reigned in the dining room.

The New Yorkers excused themselves and retreated to their quarters, ignoring him on their way out (the way New Yorkers do, as if there were nothing out of the ordinary). The mother and daughter maneuvered for the front door, explaining they wanted to watch the rising moon. The professors hung on, fidgeting with their dessert forks, wanting to escape but feeling compelled by their sense of intellectual duty to tough it out.

Dusty said, "Now, if you want to know the truth, what we have to do is wipe out all the inferior trash."

"Bullshit!" I roared, slamming down my coffee mug. The coffee sloshed and soaked the tablecloth. "That kind of racist crap breeds genocide and war—so quit it, Bub!" I wanted to climb onto the table, rally the fleeing guests, and collectively drive Dusty from the face of the earth (or at least away from here).

The professors looked back and forth at the two of us, got to their feet, and scurried toward the staircase. Lisa peeked from behind the kitchen door, but she and Heather stayed in the safe confines of the pantry. Dusty remained glowing and dominant on his dining room throne.

So infuriated I couldn't speak, I stomped out the front door, slamming the screen behind me. For a moment, I considered going back to yell some more, but I realized my anger had taken me over. I had to get control of myself. Pausing in the blackness outside the dining room window, I looked back in on the candlelit scene: Dusty's ruthless smirk had faded. He stared vacuously at the wall and Ann shook her head in despair, as if she were exhausted from dealing again with behavior that never changed.

I scaled the ladder to our woodshed loft and collapsed on our futon. Alone. Confused. Trembling with anger and fear. I needed Judi; she had always been with me at the barricades, to face life's big decisions, to help me find clarity in our marriage, to carry the other end of the mattress. Without her, I am lost.

Staring out the window into the night, I tried to find an answer to this crisis. I wanted to kill him! I couldn't afford an outright struggle, though: if the inn were turned into a battleground, that would be a victory for Dusty. Besides, in hand-to-hand combat I knew he could tear me to pieces—and we have no police on the island to save my neck. On the other hand, if I allowed him to stay he would destroy the inn's reputation, and, ultimately, me.

The moon bathed the familiar shapes in my loft, leaving everything dappled in shades of gray: no black and white, no easy way out. In the morning Dusty would have to go.

An early-rising squirrel scuttled across the roof above me. I lay on my back staring blankly at the painted ceiling. I had not slept. Inside my head I wrote a thousand scripts to humiliate him. I'd tear him apart. I'd drive him off.

The back door banged slightly: Lisa had arrived (she'd be making coffee, starting breakfast). I dreaded getting up. Pulling on my clothes, I counted the chores I'd do before confronting Dusty:

1. Check oil in generator.
2. Make sure skiff's out-haul lines hadn't twisted in the tides.
3. Carry cider up from cellar.

I made my way toward the back porch while I added to my mental list:

4. Haul drinking water from Sally's well.
5. Lug garbage to compost bin.
6. Burn trash.

I had my foot on the first step when I looked up and saw Dusty. He stood lurking on the porch, waiting for me. My left eye drifted out of focus, the way it does when I get scared. Then, adrenaline surged through my veins. "Now, listen here," I said curtly, "I can't allow you to preach your war and racism. You'll have to move on. I'll write you a check for a refund."

"You throwing me out, eh," he said.

I half expected him to spit at me.

"Look," he said, "we should talk about this."

"I don't want to talk about it," I said, launching into the litany I had rehearsed all night. "There's nothing to discuss, no room for compromise, no common ground to stand on. I won't tolerate it!" I prepared to fall to the ground beneath a barrage of karate chops.

It didn't happen, though. Instead, he stood there timidly, like a remorseful boy who had run away and come home.

His eyes were bloodshot, the corners of his mouth trembled.

"But I want to talk about it," he said.

His apparent humility caught me off-guard, leaving me without a target for my diatribe. His feet shuffled on the worn porch planks and he tried me once again. "I really *need* to talk," he said.

"Let's go down to the boathouse," I offered. We filed down to the shore in silence.

For me, my boathouse is a special place, somewhere I go when I need to reflect. Its white paint and classic proportions give it the authority of a courthouse, the comfort of a chapel. It seemed the proper place to talk to Dusty.

"I was up all night," he began, "Annie helps me through the nights . . . She encouraged me to talk to you . . . to apologize."

We sat on the workbench between the toolboxes and the chainsaw, leaning against the wall. The morning sun spilled through the window, spotlighting Dusty. No longer was he the fiery apostle of death: his face was haggard now, his eyes filled with grief. With quivering lips he explained.

"They taught me to kill. What the hell did I know? I was just an innocent kid—I thought the Marines would give me the chance to become a hero—but I got forged into a killing machine."

I had never been the audience for a soul-wrenching breakdown by a troubled veteran. I didn't know how to respond.

He went on. "Hell, an army ain't no damn good if it don't destroy everything in its path: buildings, bridges, schools, hospitals, men and women and kids. That was my job. I always did a good job, too, on everything I did—and the Corps was no exception. And they teach you to follow orders too—Christ, do they ever teach you that!"

He began sobbing uncontrollably. Tears streamed down his cheeks and spattered his pain on the embossed logo of his Nike T-shirt.

"There I was, spread-eagled in the middle of that stinkin' jungle, fighting a war that nobody back here gave a damn about," he said. "My best buddy . . . he was hunkered down there beside me . . . they blew his head apart . . . took a few seconds for his body to react before it slumped into the mud. He was only eighteen, just a poor farm kid from Louisiana. All my buddies . . . one after the other . . . what a rotten, damn shame!"

His chest heaved and the sobbing intensified.

The breakfast bell tolled from the front porch, but it sounded a million miles away, like some ancient call to arms, bringing back memories of my hatred of the war, images that haunt me still. I envisioned Dusty clad in khaki, a submachine gun in his hands . . . bullets spraying . . . him emerging in the center of my old nightmares: our soldiers at work in Vietnam; the My Lai massacre; troops throwing civilians from helicopters; the napalm, the body counts. Now Marine Dusty, with blood on his hands, had come to my house to roost.

"What the hell was I supposed to do, Jeff?" He wailed, unaware of my seething rancor. "I hated the little bastards crawling around in the dark setting booby traps and sniping. Sure, I blew away as many as I could."

I wasn't surprised.

"What was it all for?" he went on. "This country run by big-shot politicians and rich bastards only cared about dragging out the mess so they could get rich off our slaughter. Democracy? Freedom? What a crock!"

I watched him rave, but when he looked at me my gaze dropped to the floor. I didn't want him to get too close. I didn't want to care about him. The feelings were too powerful, his presence too frightening, his murderous past something I couldn't accept.

"So many kids blown into the mud," he chuckled morbidly, tears dripping from his chin. "And those who made it back got treated like lepers." He lifted his head and looked at me. "You know what, Jeff? The only ones who understand are the guys who were over there, guys who went through it with me. We sit around and get drunk and brag about how many we killed. We got nothing else to talk about! Now, ain't that the saddest damn thing you ever heard? And the only place that feels right for me is on a job like mine, another job of death."

"It might help if you tried a different occupation," I said sarcastically. It was the first thing I had said since we arrived at the boathouse. The sound of my own voice startled me; it seemed traitorous to be counseling this butcher.

"I can't change," he wailed. "I feel like a freakin' yo-yo. I wanna be good, contribute to the world, straighten myself out. But I'm as crazy as a rampaging bull, poisoned by what I've done. I blast away at whatever threatens."

Movement outside. Dusty jerked, as if frightened by the phantom of a long-ago enemy who stalked him still. It was only Annie. She brought two cups of steaming coffee. She surveyed the scene. She understood. Leaving the cups on the workbench, she gave Dusty a smile and left, never saying a word.

He watched her disappear up the path. "I love her so much," he stammered. "She's all I have. She wants me to quit the job, of course . . . move on to something else, something that doesn't anchor me to the past. I want to so much, to lead a normal life, maybe even a life like yours, Jeff, but I'm too afraid. I have to stay with my own kind."

I didn't feel much empathy.

Dusty had used his handkerchief frequently to soak up his tears. Folding the damp cloth several times, he found a dry spot and blew his nose. He became a little more controlled, exhausted from his haunting remembrances. Then his bloodshot eyes centered on me, showing curiosity. Questions formed on his face.

"What did you do, Jeff, during the war?" he finally asked.

I worried he wouldn't understand why I opposed the war his friends had died in, but after his gut-twisting performance, I felt compelled to give him an honest answer, a revelation equal to his.

I explained how, during the initial years, I never questioned the war. I was a student at Ohio State University when I witnessed my first antiwar rally in 1963. It was a feeble procession that trickled down North High Street, an unlikely harbinger of the huge demonstrations in the years to come. I remember asking one of the marchers why they were opposed to the war—I really didn't understand, I just assumed there must have been a good reason for it, like a struggle against Hitler or something. The following year Judi and I got married. We spent a year embroiled in the campus free speech movement. Then, we joined the Peace Corps in 1966, our way of acting on our youthful idealism (we had been touched deeply by President Kennedy and devastated by his death). By then we were more aware of world political realities and deeply bothered by the mounting death and destruction in Southeast Asia.

But it was our two years in Venezuela that finally made us take a stand against the war. Even in the most remote mountain valleys, barefooted peasants asked us why our government was slaughtering the Vietnamese, and why, if we believed in peace, we were representing the United States? Even more disturbing, young farmers returning to their villages from stints with the *Guardia Nacional* assumed we knew a Captain Martin or a Sergeant Harris, since we were *norteamericanos,* too (even in that bastion of South American democracy, the U.S.A. staffed and funded a significant counterinsurgency training operation to protect its "vital interests"). A few bold villagers even accused us of being agents of the CIA. We left Venezuela rich with new experiences, but with a sobering understanding of the U.S. government's determination to control the rest of the world.

As I recounted my history of growing opposition to the war, I feared Dusty might become hostile, but he listened intently, fascinated by hearing about an experience different from his own.

"Go on," he said. "Tell me more."

After Venezuela, we moved to New York City, then to California. I told Dusty how we aimed our idealism and organizing skills at new targets. We sold our house and gave the proceeds to causes we supported: the movement to abolish the Peace Corps (because of its exposed ties to the CIA), the Vietnam Veterans Against the War, the Black Panthers' breakfast program for children. In Oakland we formed a commune dedicated to building a utopian world. What wonderful years they were! We believed we had the will, the power, to bring an end to war. We were in Berkeley to cheer Jane Fonda on her return from Hanoi; we were in the human flash flood that filled the streets when the "Secret War in Cambodia" was exposed; we came with our babies and banners to the endless marches through San Francisco, to hand out leaflets at factory gates in West Oakland, to demonstrate in front of the San Francisco Stock Exchange, inside the churches, throughout the cities, until millions all around the world joined the tidal wave of opposition that finally brought an end to the madness.

When the last soldiers fled by helicopter from the roof
of the Saigon embassy we celebrated quietly. But with the
war's end our own world unraveled: the cause that shaped
our existence had dissolved. Our love children grew older.
The streets were no longer so friendly, people not so pre-
dictable, causes no longer so clearly defined. Our sense of
leading the way dissipated into trivial bickering by myriad
splinter groups. Everything fell apart. Meanwhile, blood
flowed more profusely than ever: in Central America, the
Middle East, Tiananmen Square, Africa, and Iraq, and on a
million street corners of America. I became convinced that
violence grows from the barrels of willing guns like
Dusty's, organized into armies, police forces, the paramili-
tary forces of drug lords, the contras and Khmer Rouge of
the world. They are all hachetmen for the rich.

Dusty wasn't offended by my story. In fact, he thought
there was unity in our seemingly contradictory pasts: our
lives had both been plundered by the same system, he said.

We slid off the workbench to stretch our legs, then
stood quietly in the shadows. Eventually, Dusty spoke.
"Damn it, Jeff. I wish we didn't have to go through this
crap, year after year." He wagged his head despondently.
"Why can't life be fair? We shouldn't need butchers like
me." A new wave of tears began to film his eyes.

He reached toward me with his hairy, muscular arms
and enveloped me. I wanted to push him away: these were
the arms of a murderer, one who raped and maimed and
bludgeoned old men to death. Had these tears revealed
another side, a Dusty shocked halfway sane by a life viewed
through the gun sight? I tried to relax and experience the
sensation of his body, his hands pressing against my shoulder blades, his belly flattened against mine. He sighed heavily and the rise and fall of his lungs bulged against my chest.
The faint aroma of cologne emanated from his neck. Still,

I could not accept the possibility that Dusty could be humane.

He let me loose and we stood there in the boathouse. Beneath us, the rising tide gurgled through the rocks. There was nothing left to say. We could have continued on our separate ways, two diametric opposites living a continent apart, but Dusty, having laid open his whole life's story, went on to finish mine. "So you came here to this island to create a piece of the perfect world you fought for all those years."

"I guess you could put it that way," I acknowledged. I could feel him reaching for some universal truth, some way to summarize our traumatic encounter.

"I lost my war," he said. "And you won no glorious revolution either, Jeff. You hang out here 'cause you can't hack it back in the mainstream—not much different than me, right?"

"Yup," I had to agree.

Dusty turned and stared across the water, his mind perhaps reeling with images of blazing jungles and contorted faces.

"No heroes, no parades . . . only corpses and ashes . . . only broken minds and broken dreams. No survivors on either side," he whispered, ". . . only casualties."

I was relieved two days later when Dusty and Ann finally went back to California. I never saw them again.

WHEN WE CLOSED THE INN THAT FALL, Matthew returned to high school in Blue Hill and Judi and I got back into our winter routine: writing, cross-country skiing, contra dances and potlucks at the Town Hall. In midwinter I got a note from Jay Hyland, my old friend with the Lighthouse Preservation Society, asking me to participate in a light-

house conference scheduled for the coming spring in
Washington, D.C. It seemed a splendid way to finish out the
winter.

In Washington, Jay and his colleagues had everything
well organized. The program included workshops on organizing community lighthouse preservation groups, a dedi-
cation ceremony for a series of lighthouse postage stamps,
and a "Thousand Points of Light" speech at the White
House. Fortunately, as conferences do, this one left the last
afternoon for participants to enjoy as they wished.

It was an unusually warm April day, so I went for a walk
on the Mall. I came to the Washington Monument. The tall,
sleek obelisk speared the sky in a display of grandiosity, but
I passed right by, unimpressed by its mighty height. Being
in the heartland of federal bureaucracy had already turned
my mood sour, so I felt no need to pay homage to a slave
owner, an aristocrat, a man so rich he could flaunt his
wealth by flinging a silver dollar across the Potomac.

I continued along the Reflecting Pool. At the far end
sat Abraham Lincoln, ensconced in his granite memorial,
staring up the Mall, his immortal words engraved on the
wall behind him. I walked more hurriedly as I approached,
eager to recite the address I memorized in the fifth grade.
At the base of the monument I paused to look up. He sat
looking down at America, his homely face filled with wisdom. Yet, like the Washington memorial before, this lofty
temple disappointed me: it ached with antiquity, of little
help in the modern world.

I turned and walked to my left. I wandered across a
nondescript patch of grass, past a few gaunt trees. The sun
was hot. The ground was hard against my tiring feet.

Suddenly, I came upon three soldiers dressed in battle
gear, their weapons lowered, their pained expressions cast in
bronze. No plaques explained who they were. No pedestal

raised them to lofty heights, no monumental proportions dwarfed me. We stood together, sharing the same space, the same time, the same breath of air.

I looked into their faces: boyish dreamers ripped from their proper course and sent off to take part in systematic slaughter. Their distraught eyes focused somewhere behind me. I turned to look: across the grass I saw the black wall, starting low and growing larger as it descended, following the terraced land, then rising again, a shining dark wing of death. It pulled me inextricably forward, as if I were being drawn into the grave to join a seance with the past.

The wall loomed over me; names . . . names . . . names, column after column after column of crisp carved letters covered the cold mirrored marble. Fifty-eight thousand Joneses, Riveras, Jakowskis. My eyes raced over them, fearful they might land on a name I knew. The names floated on the still, black sea with my reflection behind them, my own apparition looking back at me, marking a place that could have been mine.

Standing in the hot sun on that April afternoon, I sobbed, my dogmatic dislike for soldiers overwhelmed by feelings I'd never known before. Around me, legless veterans in wheelchairs solicited support for the P.O.W./M.I.A. cause. Others petitioned for an end to war. Park attendants rubbed impressions of names from the cold wall and presented them to widows, to now-childless mothers and now-fatherless children. And I knew that somewhere on that timeless field of stone, little clusters of letters mourned faces from throughout my life too; Dickie, the acne-cheeked kid who sat next to me in geometry class; the quiet man who drove the Long Street bus; my childhood neighbor who delivered the *Columbus Dispatch*. They were all people I'd known that I would never again see, people like Dusty . . . and people like me.

PURPLE PLUM TORTE

1 cup sugar
1/2 cup butter (unsalted)
1 cup unbleached flour, sifted
1 tsp. baking powder
2 eggs
6 ripe plums, halved and pitted
1 Tbs. lemon juice
1 tsp. cinnamon mixed with 1 tsp. sugar
1/8 tsp. nutmeg

Cream the sugar and butter. Add flour, baking powder, and eggs, and beat well. Spoon batter into greased 9-inch springform pan. Place plum halves skin side up on top of batter. Sprinkle with cinnamon/sugar mixture and nutmeg. Bake at 350 degrees for 50 minutes. Serve with vanilla ice cream or whipped cream. Guaranteed to melt the heart of the most hardened dogmatist, either left or right.

RAKING THE WOODS

12

May 18, 1990

ONCE WE'VE REOPENED IN THE SPRING and our fair-weather guests return, my renovation work on the lighthouse station ceases for the season, and it's time to groom the woods again (I like to keep the forest tidy for the creatures who live here all year round). Boreal pine voles dart between holes hidden in tangles of spruce roots. A red squirrel vaults from bough to bough. I hear the croak of the raven, the whoosh-whoosh of his wings, and a wedge of black passes above the green. Through the trees I wander with my bamboo rake, clearing away lichen-covered twigs and scales of fallen bark. Old wagon wheels, hand-blown bottles, an iron tractor seat: these are a few of the things I've uncovered. But I've found more than artifacts: I unearthed my mother's feet.

SHE DIED THE YEAR WE MOVED TO Maine. Our plans had been made, our house put up for sale, our lives redirected when the telephone rang.

"Well, Bud," said Pop, "we've got bad news . . . your mother is very ill."

In spite of her condition and her pleas for me to remain, we abandoned California, fleeing over the Rockies and shambling across the plains, our Ryder truck jammed with furniture and dogs and kids, my traitorous heart laden with guilt, a selfish son chasing dreams while his mother lay dying.

Four months later, Pop called to tell my brother, Steve, and me to hurry if we wanted to see her one last time. We caught a Delta night flight from Bangor, soaring down the eastern seaboard over Boston, New York, Baltimore, Atlanta, a milky way of urban light that swept us down the coast. We sat side by side, reminiscing about our childhood, the ways we drove her crazy, the time we threw the dummy down the stairs and scared her half to death . . . her search for her place in the sun . . . her faith in us to bloom, to learn to dream as she did. Memories, so many memories . . . running home from school for lunch . . . her welcoming smile . . . grilled cheese sandwiches and tomato soup.

It was daylight when we landed in San Francisco. We rented a car and sped north, hurtling past Candlestick Park and Hunter's Point, past Bernal Heights and Potrero Hill, spilling into the Haight and picking our way through old streets and familiar neighborhoods to the Golden Gate. Then through the hills of Marin. Highway 101 North. San Rafael. Petaluma. Santa Rosa.

Would she still be alive? What would she look like? Would she be able to speak? Would she forgive me?

Pop and our sister, Betsy, met us in the hospital waiting room. Through a maze of gurneys and nurses' stations we followed them, down a long corridor lined with open doors; Room 321 . . . 322 . . . 323 . . . 324 . . . Through each doorway I saw the foot of a bed, a motionless lump under a white cover, looping arcs of feeding tubes and oxygen lines . . . 325 . . . 326 . . . 327 . . .

Room 328. I trailed in behind my father, apprehensive, scared, yet strangely fascinated. There was Ma, all spacey and distant, draped in sheets, barely alive. She didn't know me. Past me she looked, as if I were a stranger on a city bus, her eyes reflecting some distant road to a place I wasn't a part of. Occasionally, a word . . . disconnected . . . departing.

"Rub her feet," the nurse said. "That's where she'll have feeling the longest. And talk to her. She can hear, even though she barely moves."

I stood at the end of the bed. I put my hands on her feet. No response. My fingers traced the contour of her toes and gently massaged her soles. Beneath the skin and the thin layer of flesh, the tiny bones flexed in their joints, and I remembered how they looked all strung together on the chart in biology class: the tarsus, the metatarsus, dozens of little phalanges, links in the chain that stretched from beneath my fingertips to the wilting face staring from the pillow. I tried to speak, to tell her so many things, to apologize. The words never came.

Unexpectedly, a slight movement in her throat, a twitch of her lip. Her words spilled out, as if cast by a ventriloquist, as if carried on a cleansing wind from somewhere deep inside.

"Maine lobster," she murmured with a faraway smile.

THE NEXT DAY WE FILED INTO THE CREMATORIUM. Potted ferns softened the reception area, and a few nicely upholstered chairs did what they could to lend a homey atmosphere. A friendly woman whisked in from somewhere out back and asked our names. A moment later she returned with a cardboard box, less than a cubic foot in size, wrapped tightly with cellophane tape.

"The fine crusher is broken down," she said. "We've put the remains through the coarse crusher several times, but I'm afraid they're still fairly large. If you like, we can hold them here until the other machine is fixed."

But we already had our plans: the box went in Pop's Toyota wagon and we headed for the coast. Steve drove. Pop worried about the legality of scattering her remains (he always obeys the law). We slipped away from Sebastopol and followed the country road past old dairy farms, the brown August hills of Sonoma swallowing us as we wound west toward the sea, rising and falling, twisting and turning, me in front with Steve, Pop and Betsy in back, the silent brown box in the rear.

At Goat Rock Beach we parked. Pop had brought along a day pack and struggled nervously at concealing the box, but the corners jutted stubbornly from under the flap. It was a familiar walk, her favorite, one we had all taken many times. We made our way instinctively south, past the monolithic block of stone that protrudes from the sea, along the crescent strip of sand that fades away to surf at the base of a crumbling cliff.

This was her spot. Pop went first, dipping into the box with a single hand, letting the dust and fragments fall through his fingers into the water. Then another handful. We moved a step farther out. Betsy went next. Two handfuls, sifting them into the sea, the surges coming and receiving and carrying away. Then Steve. Two more handfuls. He lofted his share a bit higher, a little farther out, the wind joining in to help him with his work.

Then it was my turn. The box was still mostly full. The six modest handfuls had hardly made a dent, so it was up to me to disperse the rest. I felt honored to do it, entitled in fact (after all, she loved me the best). I cast a handful, then another . . . and another . . . and another, the alabaster bone pattering the water's surface. The little nubs and chips felt soft in my hand, pliant and smooth and fine, as welcome as the cotton skirt she wore where I laid my head for naps. Hand by hand they disappeared, sunk to the bottom, lost forever in a world of polished pebble and broken shell. I brushed my hands together: the last clinging particles were swept away by the breeze, to the skies, to the seas, to the sands of time.

EVERYTHING MOVES IN CIRCLES. I rake the woods and marvel at the ocean, the transformation of cloud to rain to stream to sea. I watch Judi, stooped low in her garden, midwife to the herbs and vegetables in our salad bowl, their trimmings moved to the compost bin to be recycled again.

I lean on my rake and admire the spruce. They move in circles, too. From seed to sapling they grow, one day becoming fertile giants that rain their own seed across the land. Eventually, they become burdened with a few brown boughs, their branches become engorged with witch's broom, and the spread of feeding mistletoe drains away their life. Their felling grace may be a winter storm, or the roar of a chainsaw, or simply the rot of time.

Rangy roots curling everywhere, they reach from beneath the earth, always searching for something to hold. My rake clears the way, exposing these grasping naked extremities, these smooth appendages, these spreading toes . . . I see my mother's feet. I drop to my knees and reach for them, burying my hands in the dirt. The woody fiber softens, pulses, breathes in my clutch, and I can sense the bone inside, I can feel the throb of life. The smell of her oil paints drifts from her studio, and the sound of her station wagon rumbles up the drive. Sprawled on my belly, I sink lower yet into the earth, stroking her feet, holding on tight, my mouth alive with the taste of grilled cheese sandwiches and tomato soup.

MY MOTHER'S GARDEN

TOMATO SOUP

1 Tbs. olive oil
8 large vine-ripened tomatoes, cut up
1 Tbs. dried basil
1 tsp. fennel seed
pinch of sea salt
several cloves of garlic, pressed

Measure the oil into a large skillet. Add tomatoes and other ingredients. Cover and cook at high temperature for 7 minutes. Pour into blender. Process on low for a few seconds. Reheat in same skillet. Serve with jalapeño cheese grilled on sourdough. Ma always included a tall glass of cold milk. Serves 4.

GENERATOR TIME

13

A Typical August Evening, 1991

NO ELECTRICITY. NO DRONING TVS OR BLEATING RADIOS, no intercoms or ringing phones or whine of whirling motors. Only candles and gaslights. Lanterns and stars. The rising moon undiluted by the glare of city lights.

Our guests tell us over and over again, "It's like living in a fantasy land. Don't ever bring the power in." If they only knew how hard I work to keep it this way. I do my best, I swear I do, but it's been futile trying to ward off the encroachment of electricity.

My first setback occurred shortly after we moved into the lighthouse back in 1986: I wasn't permitted to install a conventional septic system.

"No dirt here," said the soil engineer, kicking at the bony earth around the station. From under his wide-brimmed hat his x-ray eyes surveyed the ground. "You got your volcanic magma, your aggregate metamorphics, your boulders left by glaciers; rock, that's all ya got. There's nothing here to absorb wastewater."

He jotted a few notes in his note-book, shaking his head in sympathy.

123

"Sorry, Cap," he said. "You'll have to install an electric sewage treatment system to pump and oxygenate and treat the stuff."

That was bad enough, but the demand to bring in power continued to mount. We had wanted to use the cellar cistern for our water supply (it's fed by rain off the roof). All we needed was a hand pump in the pantry, no expensive new plumbing, and our guests would be delighted with the frontier ambiance. We explained our plans when we filled out the application for our Maine food and lodging license.

"A cistern will never do," said the thin-lipped woman visiting from the Department of Human Services. "The likelihood for bacteria penetration is far too high, or pollution from acid rain. And what about droppings from pine voles and hairy caterpillars? I mean, there's nothing but wilderness out here! You'll have to drill a well and use a pressurized system, just like everyone else. Otherwise, there will be no license."

"Extortion!" I bellowed. "You people don't understand. This is America, where folks can do what they like! We're gonna keep things simple here."

She packed her papers quickly, wagged her head in disbelief, and rushed to catch the mailboat.

I had to face the truth: if the inn was going to succeed, I'd have to lower my standards of simplicity. Resigned to the intrusion of power, I pledged to constrain it the best I could.

One option was to sneak a power cable a half mile through the woods from my neighbors, Billy and Bernadine, but the image of lines loping through the trees and the buzzing of transformers would be an open admission of my capitulation to power.

So instead I decided on a generator. I needed one large enough to power the sewage system and the well, but small enough to be tucked away where the guests would never see it. Fortunately, I found a used rig on a neighboring island that was no longer wanted, an ugly old twin-cylinder Goliath painted institutional green. Down the bay I went with four men and brought it back in Bones McDonnell's lobster boat. We lugged it up the shore cradled in a yoke of spruce poles, like an anesthetized beast being brought to a zoo.

Accustomed to the serenity of kerosene lanterns and wood stoves, the old lighthouse station must have trembled in dismay the day we hooked up that noisy machine. We bolted it down inside a makeshift shack. I tried the starter. At first it cranked hard. Then it wheezed, coughed, and moaned, spewing smoke and water vapor. Finally, the greasy thing whirled to life and its bellicose roar filled the woods and scared the eider ducks out of the cove.

Next, I hooked up Chloressa, my turd-eating, pee-swilling sewage treatment plant, a fiberglass glutton roughly the size and shape of a Volkswagen bus. I camouflaged it with spray paint and muffled it the best I could, so guests wouldn't hear the rumble of its bowels. It has a voracious thirst for electricity, too (without adequate aeration time, it'll fail to do its job).

As soon as the pumps and sewage plant were wired, Judi decided the pantry had to have a secret outlet for a Cuisinart. Of course battery chargers were needed as well; the ship-to-shore has to be kept fully charged, as does an extra battery for Thunder's electric fence, and a few more for fluky SweetiePie, whose unpredictable short circuits leave us stranded in the woods.

Eventually I was able to concentrate these myriad electrical needs into a period I now refer to as "generator time." Generator time has to be carried out surreptitiously so as not to destroy the guests' fantasy of an island without wires.

The generator needs to be fired up as early as possible, since Judi needs power to julienne her veggies and puree her soup. It works like this: as soon as the mailboat delivers our guests and they are in their rooms freshening up, I sneak down to the generator shack to check the oil and propane bottles. Then I'm back to the cellar to throw on the master switch.

It gets a little tricky here. Heather rings the fog bell, timed just right to get folks steered into the dining room, while I disappear through the trees to flip on Chloressa. From our guests' first taste of pepper marmalade through their final bite of torte, my sewage servant needs to run all through supper to digest her daily tides of muck. As she was built to operate on a twenty-four-hour clock, I have to manually adjust her dial to get the cycles done between six and nine, stumbling through the shadowy woods many times to advance the timer.

"Gurgle, gurgle, gurgle . . ." all through soup and salad. With Chloressa muffled beyond the inn's thick walls and the dense woods, our dining guests are oblivious to her uncouth babbling and the rich odors that seep from beneath her hatches.

Then back to the cellar to plug in the battery chargers.

"Buzzzzzzzzzzzzzzzz . . ."

"Thunkity-thunkity-thunkity . . ." shake the pipes from the pumping water.

"Wheeet . . . wheeet . . . wheeet . . ." whines the pump on the chemical injector, intravenously adding soda ash and chlorine into the water tanks.

Meanwhile, above me in the dining room our guests feed on haddock with sour cream and dill. I hope their dinner conversation distracts them from all the racket.

I've wired a secret cellar light so I can carry out my evening chores. It dims . . . then brightens . . . then dims again, as the overloaded generator labors with all our needs. In the illicit flicker, I slink about pushing buttons and working levers, like the Wizard of Oz behind his billowing curtain.

Above me, the scrape and clink of silverware diminishes (the guests are done with the entree, my time is running out). I do a power check through the kitchen. Judi has her new yogurt maker plugged in (it needs another fifteen minutes), concealed in the pantry with the Cuisinart, the KitchenAid mixer, the sharpeners, blenders, and irons.

Heather serves dessert.

Back to the woods I rush, to turn Chloressa's timer.

While the guests linger over a second cup of decaf, I wait with Chloressa for the end of her last cycle. Insider her belly a ton of greasy water, black suds, crumbling feces, and soggy toilet paper churn, surging against her sides while her air pipes gulp from the darkening skies.

I'm so tired. I lean against Chloressa, the broad curve of her tank just right to support my weary back, the pulsing vibrations of her pumps soothing my muscles, the biodegrading heat inside warming me through her walls. We are conspirators in the night, my machine and me: we labor secretly to fight back the march of time, to generate an illusion of simplicity for these seekers from the cities.

Finally, the last gush of gray water is gone. I turn off Chloressa so she can rest for the night. By the end of the evening I'm exhausted, too, from racing back and forth. Gosh, keeping things simple takes a lot of work!

My feet know the way back through the familiar ledges, even on a moonless night. I stumble into the fans of candlelight spilling from the windows. Inside, I make my final rounds. Is the yogurt done? Are the gadgets unplugged? I descend one last time to the cellar. I shut down the battery chargers, the hidden lights. Are the pressure tanks full? The compressor off?

Now I wait wearily in my command post beneath the
dining room. I know dinner is over when I hear the screech
of chairs being pushed back on the bare wood floor. Gay
voices drift toward the front door as guests make their way
out to look at the stars. Just in time, I throw the main circuit breaker, and as the screen door squeaks open, the last
telltale groan from the generator shack is swallowed by the
night.

In spite of resounding customer satisfaction, occasionally some politically correct purist picks on me for my
shenanigans (one guidebook author even accused me of
defrauding my guests by pretending no electricity exists
here). But I'd like to think I'm providing a refuge from the
frantic world out there, where stressed-out folks can rest
and procreate more mild-mannered offspring. So even if
my petty crimes are exposed by the glow of Chloressa's
control panel or the whine of water pumps vibrating within the walls, why vilify me for simplifying this noble work
with a sputtering generator? Like my counterpart from Oz,
I'm not a bad man; I'm just an incompetent wizard.

HADDOCK WITH SOUR CREAM
AND DILL

1/4 tsp. thyme
I Tbs. dill weed or I tsp. dried dill weed
1/2 tsp. sugar
1/4 tsp. salt
1/4 tsp. pepper
I cup sour cream
paprika
2 pounds haddock

Mix together all ingredients except fish and paprika. Place pieces of fish in a buttered casserole dish. Spread sour cream over fish. Sprinkle with paprika. Bake for 25 minutes at 350 degrees. Serves 6. It's simple and delicious, just what you need when the world seems complex and overwhelming.

14

WALKING STICKS
Three Case Studies of an Everyday Occurrence

Summer 1991

A FEW WEATHERED WALKING STICKS LOOK CUTE leaning against the front of the Keeper's House (it's the quaint country look, like decoys, wagon wheels, and baskets of dried flowers). Individually chosen by our guests while trekking along the shore, each staff retains a bit of soul from the person who left it here. But, invariably, when the mailboat pulls away, these walking sticks are left behind, orphaned, deserted—on *my* front porch. I'd like to take care of them, I really would, but I don't know what to do with so many: they keep piling up, like the mountains of logs at the Bucksport paper mill. I can't burn them or toss them to the tides—my conscience won't allow it. If only there were someone else to dispatch them! Unfortunately, like it or not, the responsibility for dealing with them does fall on my shoulders: after all, I am the innkeeper.

It's easy to understand why guests pick them up. This is a treacherous island to hike, rugged and wild and scarce of soil. Beneath the emerald skirt of vegetation lies bedrock born from volcanic cauldrons. After the magma hardened, the laborious passing of gla-

131

ciers scoured and shaped it. Eons passed, ice melted. Granite
boulders and the refuse of foreign shores were left behind,
the land became flooded, and only the tip of this mountain
we know as Isle au Haut remained above the sea. Then
came millennia of freezing ocean spray and scorching sun,
aging the island with crevices and crumbling cliffs. Not
much loam ever evolved, only enough to support the gaunt
spruce that cling to this broken heap of rock, and the bayberry bushes and beach grasses that wave along the shore.
In more recent ages, hikers have worn a few trails here and
there, linking the harbors and valleys and our little town.
They are primitive paths, booby-trapped with snares of
roots and ledges covered with slippery moss, an obstacle
course which causes twisted ankles and broken legs. A
proper walking stick is a necessity.

Although I've dealt with an army of abandoned sticks,
each has been unique and each has a story to tell. Here are
just a few.

PETER AND DAVYNE SET THE STANDARD for walking-stick
aesthetics. They visit every summer from Connecticut. He
is a painter; she, a poet. For them, selecting a walking stick
is an artistic endeavor. Their staffs must be properly propor-
tioned, aged to a rich patina, and polished like jewels by
wind and surf. Once they've arrived at their favorite cove
(they call it "the studio"), Peter fashions a serviceable easel,
using his boot laces to lash together their walking sticks
with other bits of driftwood. Then, his strokes commence.
The sun arcs overhead and sweat pours from his brow, fierce
little rivulets that fog his bifocals and spatter his palette,
adding a bit of salt to his pigment. He splashes wildly with
color. The skies and seas and rock take root on his canvas,
as if a hunk of the shore had broken loose and drifted there.

Davyne lounges naked at the water's edge. Big and round and smooth as the boulders where she lingers, she sips Beaujolais and writes eleven-line sonnets, providing a Rubenesque focus for Peter's flailings. Later, on the front porch, their walking sticks stand aloof from all the other staffs, their perfect form and the telltale spatter of paint setting them apart.

THE STORIES OF OUR GUESTS' WALKING STICKS aren't always so idyllic.

I'll never forget the April morning our Brooklyn friends Franny and Silverstein hiked up the shore and carried back Matilda. They thought she was an exhausted sea turtle searching for the ocean. With a piece of fishnet that Franny found mired in the rockweed they rigged a litter between their walking sticks. By this means they managed to lug the lethargic reptile back to the lighthouse, a snaggle of legs and twine. Silverstein started to stroke the turtle's head, hoping he could rouse it from its torpor.

"Come on, Matilda, wake up, sweetheart. You'll be all right," he coaxed, scratching her under the chin, the way you pleasure a puppy. His fumbling seemed only to entangle the poor creature further.

Eddie, the island naturalist, looked up from tinkering with SweetiePie's alternator, his long beard festooned with little braids and colored beads. He lives on an eternally mastless schooner moored in the Thorofare, occasionally working at the inn whenever I call for help with an internal combustion machine. When he saw Franny and Silverstein wrestling with the entangled turtle, he put aside his screwdriver and came to lend a hand.

Having managed finally to free the creature, Silverstein had gotten down on his hands and knees to frolic with his

new playmate when Eddie came close enough to identify
the species. Eddie's eyes bulged out in terror.

"Watch out!" he screamed. "That's a snapper!"

Silverstein jerked back. "Yikes!" he exhaled, leaping
free. He quickly inventoried his fingers, just to make sure
that none had been pruned away.

Carefully, we studied the prehistoric spiny shell, the
robotic movements of plated legs pawing at the gravel, the
diabolical glare of its red eye, the yawning, steely beak fashioned for breaking bone and tearing meat. A snapping turtle has no need to retract inside a shell: its armor is thick,
its weaponry deadly.

After Eddie conjectured that the turtle was waking from
its winter hibernation, Silverstein felt badly about having
removed it from its habitat. He is a conscientious fellow, and
now he felt responsible for helping Matilda find a suitable
freshwater marsh. He nudged it toward the woods with his
walking stick. Franny took pictures. After a few gentle prods,
the snapper stirred to life and took a bead on Silverstein's
staff. A hissing snarl erupted. Then its beak lashed out, and
soon the end of the staff became a frazzle of shredded pulp.

With its reptilian eyes afire and its scaly neck flexing,
Matilda stood defiantly before us, daring us to approach.
(An enraged snapping turtle, I'd once read, can tear apart a
dog.) Ed and I managed to snare it with the rig of net and
walking sticks. Guardedly, we lugged it down to Aubrey's
swamp and set it beside the bog. It glared at us meanly and
gave a final hiss. Its dinosaur claws scrabbled at the earth
and it launched itself into the muck. There was a swirl of
muddy bubbles, a ripple through the weeds, a crest of shimmering water, and then it was gone. Now, each time I pass
Aubrey's swamp, I proceed with caution: there's always a
chance that Matilda may be lurking there waiting for a
chance to get even. The walking stick? When Franny and

Silverstein departed, it became just another homeless
vagrant inhabiting my front porch, its tip frazzled, shredded,
ripped asunder by Matilda's attack.

NOT ALL THE WALKING STICKS left in my care are branded
with paint or scars. Most merely stand as reminders of those
who leave them here. One by one, they are deposited by
courting lovers, honeymooners, and couples celebrating
anniversaries. Some folks even come here to be married.
This summer, Paul brought Diana here just to propose.

He planned the event for months.

"I want the most romantic room," he said, the day he
called Mrs. Robbins in Stonington to make his reservations
(our telephone is six miles away on the mainland). "Reserve
the rest for my friends, my best man, my brother, my sister,
and her husband. I want them all there to share my joy
when I pop the question to Diana."

"Jeff and Judi will help you get it organized," said Mrs.
Robbins. "They love these special occasions."

We certainly do. I really got into it. I called Paul the
next time I was off-island and we planned the whole event.

"Let's use the boathouse for the proposal site," I suggested. "On a starry night with the seas gurgling underneath, it's the perfect spot."

His excitement flushed across the phone line.

"I want the works," he said. "Maybe some flowers,
roses, red ones. And champagne, the best you can get. And
candles, too. Everything should be just right. This will be
the most important moment of my life."

We spent weeks getting ready. Judi organized a special
dinner. It was my responsibility to set the stage in the
boathouse and coordinate the drama. As soon as Paul and
Diana checked in, he'd lead her up the shore for a walk,

away from the boathouse so I could set it up. Then would
come Judi's feast of homemade pasta with lobster sautéed in
garlic and rum, something that would really warm Diana
up. After dinner, he would invite her for a stroll down to
the boathouse. I would have everything ready: a vase of
roses on the workbench, a flaming candelabra, an uncorked
bottle of Dom Perignon chilling in a bucket of seawater. In
the seaward doors, I'd have my two ratty workshop chairs
pushed together facing the lighthouse. Paul's sister would
bring a cassette player with Diana's favorite tune, "Lara's
Theme," from *Doctor Zhivago*. It would be hidden under the
workbench where Paul could flip it on at the proper
moment. His brother was in charge of the next morning's
breakfast toast, a salute to the coming wedding and wishes
for a prosperous marriage.

The day they arrived, the entire station pulsed with
energy. Diana was a vibrant young woman with flashing
eyes that never looked away. Her skin was faintly dark, hint-
ing of some exotic race mixed in her blood, and the honey-
colored hair draped around her shoulders rolled in waves
every time she laughed. She dressed provocatively in a
breezy summer blouse and tight jeans, padding barefoot
around the inn. A small gap between her front teeth was her
only imperfection, a distinctive feature that made her even
more seductive. The women watched her with measured
admiration; the men with obvious desire. Paul's eyes never
left her. He fussed over her, catered to her wishes, followed
behind her wherever she went, forever dragging with him
an attaché case containing honeymoon brochures, notes for
his proposal speech, and a glittering diamond ring.

Judi and Lisa started dinner. While the rest of the party
lounged in front of the lighthouse, Paul and Diana went for
their walk. An hour later, they returned, climbing through the
rocks with the aid of a newly acquired pair of walking sticks.

"Matched ones," Paul said to me proudly, showing off the weathered staffs. "I found two identical ones." He winked at me when he said that and wiggled his ring finger when she wasn't looking, alluding to the pair of matched wedding bands he had picked out at Tiffany's. He looked hungrily at Diana, who stood smoldering beside him. (How difficult it must have been not to propose on the spot!)

I rang the fog bell. Paul, Diana, and all their friends and family filed into the dining room. While Heather served, I sneaked down to the boathouse. Buster had brought the roses on the late boat, the champagne the day before. In the dining room, anticipation thickened. Paul was beside himself, pouring wine for everyone and doting over Diana. From the kitchen, Judi, Lisa, Heather, and I strayed past the dining room every chance we got, just to soak up a bit of the excitement that was percolating there.

Finally, dessert was done. I made my dash to the boathouse to uncork the champagne and light the candles. The scene was set.

A moment later, Paul leaned over to Diana and whispered. "How about a little after-dinner promenade?" he cooed.

She blushed, reached over, squeezed his thigh. "Sure, sweetheart," she said. She pushed back her chair and rose. The future best man, the brother, the sister and her husband, all of us in the kitchen, we all sighed and smiled and watched them leave, the screen door slamming softly behind them. Then, we all went to bed.

In the morning, the kitchen sizzled with excitement. Judi wanted to see the ring. Heather had a million questions: Would they return to the Keeper's House for the wedding? Where would they honeymoon? Was she nervous? Did she cry?

One by one, Paul's friends and family jaunted down and took their seats at the breakfast table. Heather poured juice. Judi pried loose piping hot peach-raspberry muffins from the baking tins and sent them off to the dining room. In celebration of the event, she had baked an extraordinary quiche Lorraine, blended with fresh herbs from the garden. As soon as it came out of the oven, she laced its umber crust with calendula petals and wild clover.

Then, Diana descended. While she dallied in the foyer fussing with her hair, Judi sent Heather into the dining room with a slice of quiche for each place setting. Everyone was waiting.

Diana entered, moved to the coffee urn, and filled her cup with decaf. She reached for the cream and dribbled a bit into her cup. She added a half-teaspoon of sugar. She stirred it. We all strained for a glimpse at her ring finger. Finally, she turned toward her companions, moved to the table, sat down. Paul had still not appeared.

An hour later, Heather cleared the table. Some of the plates were clean, but most contained food only partially eaten. Paul's was never touched; his slice of quiche lay pale and cold, the flower petals limp, their color fading. Upstairs, the gaiety of the previous night had changed to hushed murmurs and the sounds of luggage being packed. From the window, I watched Paul trail sorrowfully down the front porch steps. He disappeared into the woods, accompanied only by the cold, lonely presence of a solitary walking stick.

GUESTS COME, GUESTS GO. Not a dirty sock or dog-eared novel is left behind to mark the time they spend here. Only a front-porch thicket of walking sticks remain, an ever-growing disarray of flotsam that creates safety problems and fire hazards.

I finally found a solution, though. Every few weeks I gather up most of the walking sticks (leaving a few because they do look kind of nice). Then I lug them by the bundle into the woods. In a thick grove at the bottom of Bald Mountain, I arrange them in a circle around an old bull spruce, propped in the spiny dead growth of the lower limbs. Here, these abandoned walking sticks stand together through the ages, a monument to the folks who briefly touched them, a remembrance of intimate conversation, of grand plans fulfilled or thwarted, of relationships maturing or run aground forever on the shoals of broken dreams.

LOBSTER WITH RUM AND

HOMEMADE PASTA

2 Tbs. olive oil
2 cloves garlic, minced
meat from 2 steamed lobsters, cut into chunks
2 Tbs. dark rum
juice of 1 lemon and 1 lime
4 chopped scallions
1 tsp. fresh or 1/4 tsp. dried dill
1 tsp. fresh or 1/4 tsp. dried tarragon
1/2 tsp. pepper
1/2 cup heavy cream

Heat oil in heavy skillet and brown garlic over high heat. Add lobster meat
and cook for one minute. Add all ingredients except cream. Stir. Stir in
cream and heat gently. Serve over homemade pasta—if you like to make
it. (See below.) Otherwise, use Prince brand. Serves 4 generously.

HOMEMADE PASTA

Turn on your generator and run an extension cord to your Cuisinart. Use
1 1/3 cups flour and 2 eggs. Spin for 60 seconds. Feed dough through
pasta machine, or roll out on floured surface and cut noodles by hand.

15

THE BOAT LANDING—PART 2
Billy Breaks the News

January 18, 1992

EVERY WINTER THE WEATHER CHANNEL on my VHF radio
crackles with warnings of nasty arctic storms moving in.
They dump their snow on Bangor, more than seventy miles
north, or blow themselves dry over open water. We get their
drifting banks of snow, of course, their gusty winds and
rolling swells, but it's been over thirty years since the last *real*
storm struck. Testimony to its devastation, all around
Lighthouse Point stretches a perimeter of raw stone, a no-
man's land between sea and woods, where no loose boulder
or clump of clover or single grain of dirt remains, just the
sun-bleached bone of bedrock clawed bare by raging seas.

Our summer guests see only gentle waters. When they
begin arriving in May, they find a bay that coos like a baby.
Then, during June and July, the ocean reposes lazily. Only
if the weather backs around to the northwest or a strong
onshore gale sends swells bulldozing up
the Thorofare do we suffer a few days of
rolling seas.

By late summer, the ocean is
comatose. Only the rise and fall of tides
remind us this is not a lake. As the sun
sinks in the sea, our guests linger by the

141

lighthouse snacking on hummus and sparkling cider, waiting to feast on Judi's marinated chicken breasts, marveling
at the burning western sky. They are unaware of the migration of the sunsets they watch. After the summer solstice
passes, each evening the embers sink a degree farther south
down the swarthy profile of the Camden Hills. The sea feels
the tightening, the pinching of warmth between twilight
and dusk. Her moodiness grows, her surface more frequently furrowed with cutting waves. At night, a stone
thrown into the cove creates an eruption of late-summer
phosphorescent plankton, the concentric ripples glistening
like bursting fireworks.

As autumn passes, the water discolors to gunmetal gray.
Falling temperatures and changing winds whip the steely
sea into a fury of whitecaps. By late October, on windy
days our float pitches dangerously. I have to wave off the
mailboat and take SweetiePie to fetch our guests from the
village, where *Mink* finds more protected dockage.

Although major storms rarely hit the island, a full-
blown autumn storm could cause disasters, so I take sensi-
ble precautions. When the VHF calls for weather that could
threaten my landing, here's what I do: first, I recruit guests
to man the boathouse winch. We haul the ramp onto the
pier, the skiff ashore. The shore lines to the float I cast off,
letting it ride out the weather on its moorings. Once everything is battened down, I go to bed secure, confident that I
can sleep safely through the weather.

Outside, the storm intensifies. The howl of the wind is
relentless and the surf fills the night with a constant droning rumble. Judi purrs beside me. I am safe and warm
beneath my blankets, but I cannot sleep. I lie awake and
worry that maybe this time, this year, will come the Big
Storm. Inevitably, in the middle of the night I reach
through the blackness for my flashlight (I know by habit

where it lies). I sit on the edge of the bed and haul on my jeans. Judi rolls over to fill my space.

Barefoot and drowsy, I stumble out the door. Shrieking wind. Ocean roar. Creaking spruce wailing in the darkness. The ocean's thunder shakes me awake and the cold wind off the water strips away my bedroom warmth, while my flashlight struggles to light a tunnel through the trees; the night seems too vast and too mean to be illuminated. I follow the oval spit of light as it sweeps the path before me. Near the shore, the wind is even stronger. Trees quake in the darkness around me, fearful behemoths whose shallow roots tremble beneath the forest floor, trying to hang on through one more storm.

I duck into the boathouse. Though the old building squeaks and groans, the heavy timbers and worn plank floor provide a peaceful sanctuary, a respite from the wind. At the seaward end, the wide double doors are held closed by a two-by-four; I knock it loose, the doors pop outward, the wind catches them, jerks them from my grasp, flings them wide open, crashes them against the outside of the building.

I lean into the wind. Its peppery cold makes me squint. It whips my hair and tries to force me back. There is no protection from it here, no lighthouse walls, no quilted blanket, not even a scrub of beach pea to break the breath of this gale. I raise my wand of light to force back the howling darkness, but the beam is broken, diffused, lost in the spray.

Around me, the sea thunders and boils. Torrents rain down, leaving the deck slick, cold beneath my naked feet. Gripping the handrail, I creep onto the pier. Where is the float? Is it still here? As the rollers crash on the ledges before me, my flashlight catches their toothy white ridges; they stampede toward me, thundering monsters of muscle and power. At the height of their lunging, they strike the pier

with such aggression the steel **I**-beams beneath me quiver.
What a struggle to hold my light against this violence!
Finally, my beam finds a ghostly image of the float, tossing
in the dark ocean valleys, still riding on its moorings.

Cold, wet, shivering, I retreat to my bed. Sleeping Judi
senses my return and makes room for me. I curl into the
warm spot beside her. The perfume of her body and the
sounds of her breathing soothe me as I try to sleep, but the
distant drone of the sea keeps me awake. My float won't be
safe until the storm is over.

In a day or two, after the sea regains her composure, we
will launch the skiff again. I'll call once more for my guests
—another set now, the others since departed. Fresh arms
will turn the winch, lower the ramp, haul the float tight to
its berth. And once again the boat landing will greet visitors, new ones, oblivious to the storm that passed.

By the end of October, we disassemble the landing for
the winter. The ramp is winched onto the pier and lashed
securely. We haul the float ashore in the cove to dry and wait
for spring. Stripped of float and ramp, the barren pier hun-
kers among the rocks through the winter, besieged by the
harshest storms. Ice chunks hammer the pilings. Vicious seas
chew at the boathouse door. By mid-January, the freezing
spray slathers up the pilings until the pier is encased in ice.

YEAR AFTER YEAR, I GO THROUGH THE SEASONS with my
boat landing. Each passing storm teaches me more. During
the night, I listen to the pitch of the wind and watch the
spruce stir the stars and feel the cadence of the breakers
beating the shore; they tell me how much punishment my
pier is taking. When daylight returns, I stand in the cover of
the boathouse and watch the pier sway and the float jerk,
torn between crashing surf and sucking undertow.

In the winter of 1992–93 we moved to Orland on the mainland for Matthew's junior year in high school. For Christmas vacation, Judi and I took a driving trip across the country to San Francisco to see Peter, Dawn, and all our old friends. Matthew flew out to join us. On our way home, as we covered the last link north from Boston, a nasty nor'wester overtook us, caking the roads with ice and pummeling us with windy punches that jostled our usually surefooted Toyota camper. I drove haltingly, the slanting snow beating against the windshield, my eyes glazing over from staring at swirling bleakness, the drifting snow queasy beneath my tires. It was so treacherous I wanted to stop, but the plowed berm of snow packed high along both sides of the road left nowhere to pull over. When we reached the top of Snowball Hill north of Camden, we found the view across Penobscot Bay obscured by the storm. I worried about my pier.

Judi sensed my tension.

"I did everything I could before we left," I said, answering her unvoiced concern.

The Boston Globe had carried a dire weather forecast: not only was the nor'wester packing seventy-mile-an-hour winds, but the moon tide was extreme, bringing fourteen feet of water to threaten the coastal zone.

"My stomach hurts," I said.

"Jeffrey, there's nothing you can do now. I'm sure the pier will be all right; it's built of steel, and designed to last for ages. Stop your needless worrying—enjoy the pretty weather."

While we crept along Lincolnville Beach, a mighty blast of arctic wind slammed against us, the Toyota sliding perilously sideways on the unsanded road. To our right, the bay seethed. Looking outward toward Isle au Haut, I saw only a vast emptiness of wind-driven snow.

An hour later, we were back in Orland. I picked up the
phone immediately and called Billy, broadcasting by micro-
wave via Stonington. I imagined him sitting there in his
La-Z-Boy in front of his window, watching the lighthouse
between his stocking feet, his Defiant woodstove raging,
Bernadine there behind him, boiling corned hake. He
reported on the storm.

"Worst I've ever seen, and I been livin' here goin' on
fifty-seven years now," he said. "Tide some wicked high,
topped with twelve-foot rollers sweepin' 'round the point."

"How's my pier?" I asked.

"Well . . . ," he paused, "it's gone."

THE NEXT DAY, I STOOD ON THE SHORE by the boathouse.
Low tide. Skies crusted with a residue of crumbling clouds.
The wind had fallen out, but a cannonade of breaking seas
still thundered from the passing storm. Before me lay the
broad margin of black rock exposed by the falling tide,
shrouded in rockweed, littered with twisted beams from my
pier, like crumpled bodies on a battlefield. Shards of my
aluminum ramp lay strewn among the barnacles and peri-
winkles. The float, left high on the cobble beach in the cove
last fall, now sat in Thunder's pasture, and the thousand tons
of stone beneath it had been churned and tumbled a fath-
om further inland.

THAT SUMMER, WE HAD NO BOAT LANDING. SweetiePie
held up heroically, making at least two trips a day to the
Town Landing to fetch guests and supplies. But it wasn't the
same without our dock: its presence had become an inte-
gral part of life at the lighthouse station. It would have to
be rebuilt.

One thing was clear: after watching the landing flex and creak for all those years, I knew now how to build it better. I drew a set of plans. In them, I included these improvements:

- Build the pier four feet higher above mean high tide.
- Weld angle iron cross-bracing between the legs.
- Relocate the leg's pinning points on the broadest, most massive ledges.
- Tie the carrying beams into the rock with steel rod.
- Shorten the pier by ten feet on each end, leaving a smaller, higher target.
- Replace the first ten feet of pier with a knock-down wood bridge that can be moved in advance of onshore storms.
- Compensate for the outside ten feet with a longer, heavier ramp.
- Add extra shore lines and heavier mooring chains to the float.

It took the rest of the year to get the new pier built. It's higher, shorter, stronger, more versatile. Will it last a little longer? Will it take the hurricanes, bore tides, vicious nor'westers, the battering of ice floes, the stress of surge and undertow hammering, the eroding effect of oxidation, electrolytic action, solar baking, and arctic freezing? We are on a battlefield here, a zone of conflict between man and nature, where only the most hearty feel at home: the raven and seal, the mink and whale, and my neighbors Billy and Bernadine.

"It's a hard place to keep a pier," Billy always reminds me.

MARINATED CHICKEN

BREASTS

6 whole boneless chicken breasts, halved
1/4 cup lemon juice
4 tsp. Worcestershire sauce
4 tsp. garlic salt
2 cups sour cream
4 tsp. celery salt
2 tsp. paprika
1/2 tsp. pepper
1 3/4 cups bread crumbs
1/4 cup melted butter mixed with 1/4 cup melted shortening

Mix together all ingredients except chicken, bread crumbs, and butter mixture. Place in large bowl, add chicken, and make sure it is well covered. Marinate at least 12 hours. Roll chicken in bread crumbs. Arrange chicken in single layer in shallow baking dishes. Spoon half of butter mixture over chicken. Bake uncovered 45 minutes at 350 degrees. Spoon on rest of butter mixture. Bake another 10 to 15 minutes. Serves 12. The perfect entrée for a jag of hungry folks on a dark and stormy night.

16

WINDOWS

A Clear, Dry Day in June 1992

EVERY SPRING I PAINT ONE SIDE of the Keeper's House. Each side has four windows. Each window has six lights in the top sash, six in the bottom. That adds up to forty-eight panes per side. The storm sash match the windows, so actually there are ninety-six panes per side. For all four sides, including the cellar sash, the entry doors, and the windows in the gable ends, the number swells to four hundred eighty-six.

Then, of course, there are the attendant buildings: the barn and woodshed (one hundred seventy-four panes), the boathouse (sixty-three panes), Matt's shack (twenty-two), the oil house (forty-eight), and the outhouse (three). Seven hundred ninety-six glazings in all. Each pane is set apart by a thin muntin that holds the glass and putty. With four sides to a pane, there are three thousand one hundred ninety-six muntin edges to be scraped, primed, reputtied, primed again, then top-coated; fifteen thousand nine hundred eighty surfaces.

That's for the outsides. The insides are easier; no putty, less scraping, and a single priming before the top coat, only

149

an additional nine thousand five hundred eighty-eight separate little tasks. Grand total: twenty-five thousand five
hundred sixty-eight.

Then come the casing, jambs, and sills. Their surfaces
are broad and flat, asking only for a bit of refastening and
the snug comfort of fresh caulk (that's assuming the flash-
ings are sound and the accompanying soffits, cedar gutters,
and rake boards are in good repair). Occasionally a bleeding rusty nail or a punky board needs to be replaced, or a
frayed sash cord may part and require the casing to be pried
off, the runaway weight to be fished out of the wall and
refitted with new rope, and the whole works reassembled.
Then: scrape, prime, paint.

Once my windows are prepped and the sash slide
freely, they perform an elemental symphony: the dry scraping of wood against wood, the hollow clanking of balance
weights as they rise and fall within the walls, the squealing
of sash pulleys with a century of rust and paint crusting
their joints. Their voices carry through the house like a
grapevine of old friends sharing secrets, stories about the
keepers' families who lived here through the years, recalling
the sounds of love, of rage, of children growing up and old
people dying. I leave them free to gossip; to silence them
with oil would be an affront to their wisdom and dignity.

Built high on a promontory, our lighthouse station has
a view from every window, water around us everywhere,
rocky islands hunkering across the horizon with fringes of
forest softening their edges. These old panes, pockmarked
with dimples and wrinkled with waves, play games with the
surroundings, causing them to undulate, tricking us with
illusions, creating landscapes for a children's book of fairy
tales. At night the rose-colored blink of the lighthouse tints
the glass and teases the bedrooms with pulses of blushing
light.

And when the wind blows, the sash shake. During the day we go about our work oblivious to the rattling, busy maintaining the grounds and cooking meals, the aroma of Judi's honey wheat bread wafting from the kitchen window to tease woodland creatures and arriving guests. But at night, when eyes press closed and breathing slows, the old house whispers hypnotically, the prevailing breeze nuzzling the glass and making the sash rattle like dreamy castanets, a serenade that lulls us to slumber and leaves the house alone to enjoy its haunting music.

This spring I am painting the south side of the house. By early June the preparation is finally done, but all the weeks spent replacing rotten wood and scraping and putty-ing and priming have been only a prelude for the culmi-nating accent of the ladder, the blazing finale, my glorious application of bright white paint.

I awake to the perfect day: dry air, gentle breeze, tem-pered sun. It's the one I've been waiting for, the day I give my windows their final coat. I ready my ladders. I mix the paint. The creamy liquid gleams in the can and laps eagerly at the stick as I stir. The basement and first-floor windows I leave for last (they are easy, within reach from the ground or from a short stepladder). The second-floor windows are high, worthy of caution and careful planning. Their time will come another day.

This day, the most perfect of all, is saved for me to soar; I begin with the very highest, the tiny gable windows, the forty-foot extension ladder straining to reach them, their distant glass shimmering in the peaks. With my favorite sash brush clenched in my teeth and the paint can gripped in one hand, I climb.

At the top I hang my bucket from the highest rung, the ladder trailing away from me downward, a silvery beanstalk vanishing into the distance, back to the world from where

I came. The onshore breeze makes my willowy perch sway.
Synchronized in an aerial ballet, as nimble as a ladybug on
a blade of blowing grass, I cling to my place in the sky. I am
meant to be here, at the top of this ladder, surrounded by
swaying tops of tall spruce and tumbling puffs of clouds and
the sea with her breast laced with ledges awash in spray.

This is my finest moment. I dip my brush. Just the right
amount of paint. Then, the perfect stroke, the precise angle
of application, the proper pressure against the sash. Blazing
white, my paint flows over the muntins, each slender splinter nourished by the milk I give, the glass barely kissed by
my ivory trails. Exact strokes. Four times per pane. Twenty-
four times per sash. Forty-eight times per window. Then the
stiles, the rails, the casing and jambs.

Overhead the fish hawk soars, chirping wildly, scolding
me for invading its space. Lobster boats crisscross the bay,
their drone merging with the slosh of seas that play against
the shore. But I hear only the caress of bristle against wood,
and I smell only the aroma from my pail, and I feel only the
pull of the brush, and I see only white paint, straight lines,
sharp angles.

Windows . . . wood windows . . . old wood windows . . .

HONEY WHEAT BREAD

1 Tbs. yeast
2 1/2 cups warm water
1 tsp. salt
1/2 cup honey
1/3 cup molasses
1/3 cup margarine
4 cups white flour
2 1/2 cups whole wheat flour
1 1/2 cups rye flour

Dissolve yeast in water in a large bowl. Add salt, honey, molasses, margarine, 1 1/2 cups white flour, and all the wheat flour. Beat. Add all the rye flour and 1 1/2 cups white flour. Knead in rest of flour, about 10 minutes. Place dough in greased bowl. Cover. Let rise for 1 1/2 hours. Punch dough down. Put in three small greased bread pans. Let rise until doubled. Bake 40 minutes at 350 degrees.

17

AT HOME WITH DAN
AND NANCY

December 1992

EVERY AUGUST DAN AND NANCY RETURN to the Keeper's House for their annual summer vacation, driven from the bowels of New York City by murder, rape, and mayhem. With their canvas grips and the huge sail bag that contains their fold-up kayak, they leap joyously from the mailboat, thankful to be back on the island. During their stay at the lighthouse, they relate gruesome tales of city terror.

"Why don't you stay and live in Maine?" I always ask.

Dan and Nancy wag their heads, as if I couldn't understand. "Who would man the barricades at work?" they say. "We're needed there, to keep the city alive. What would happen to America if everyone fled the cities?"

On departure day, they board *Mink* reluctantly, hauling their kayak in behind them and shouting invitations for us to visit. Why, I wondered, would they relish hosting us if all they do is fend off muggers?

I decided to find out. In mid-December of 1992, after our fall chores were done and the inn was sealed for the winter, Matthew and I took off for a Manhattan weekend.

While Matthew drove our rusty Toyota pickup down
the interstate through a downpour, I closed my eyes and
reminisced about my first visit to the city, more than thirty
years before. I was only seventeen, the same age as Matthew
now. At the end of a Cape Cod summer, I had driven my
Chevy convertible through the Holland Tunnel on my vir-
ginal expedition to the Big Apple, escorted by Ray Brock,
an artist friend I had met on the beaches of Truro. He put
me up in his warehouse studio in the East Village, a cathe-
dral-like room at the top of a steep wooden staircase (there
was an elevator, but it didn't work). A mattress on the floor,
an ugly refrigerator housing solvents and brushes, an old
cast-iron sink spattered and streaked with paint, an iron-
stained toilet in the corner; these were his only furnishings.
When he left to visit friends, I stretched out on his bed.

Amid his easels and half-painted nudes, I fantasized
about the seductive images around me. Exhausted by the
long drive, lulled by the aroma of oil paint and the glint of
bright sunlight flooding through the windows, I became so
drowsy I drifted away. I don't know how long I slumbered,
but eventually the slam of the warehouse door awakened
me: a naked young woman with flowing waves of raven
hair appeared, moving among the easels as if she had come
to life from out of the paintings. She crossed the room and
sat on the toilet in front of me. I can't remember what she
said: I was too groggy with sleep, too mesmerized by her
brown Mediterranean beauty, her sculpted nakedness, the
sound of her pee streaming into the toilet. She smiled. She
wiped. She flushed. She glided past me, her bare feet
padding by so closely I could have reached out and touched
them. Behind her, the door swung closed, and only the
musky sweetness of turpentine remained. Sheets of light fell
through the high windows and made the air sparkle, leaving an aura of silvery dust swirling around the john.

"Wake up, Dad. We're almost there."

I took over the driving and we bounced along the pot-hole-riddled Cross-Bronx Expressway, across the Triboro, into Manhattan. The rain fell harder. Gutters ran like rivers. Radio announcements called for gale-force winds and record rain-falls. On Broadway, pedestrians turned their umbrellas into shields, lowering them to fend off pellets of wind-driven water that blew like bullets through the city canyons.

Dan and Nancy wouldn't be home until evening, but we wanted to drop off our gear and park the car, so we found their apartment on Seventh Street in the Village. We got the key from the doorman, rode up in the elevator, managed to figure out the jumble of locks, pushed open the door, and walked in. They have no children and no expensive avocations, so I expected their apartment to be spacious and furnished exotically, reflecting their international interests.

But it was a tiny place. A smallish living room, a cramped bedroom, a slash in the wall for a kitchenette, a bathroom with hardly room to turn around—that was all there was, all made more claustrophobic by mountains of books everywhere. Bookshelves covered every wall, with oversized volumes laid sideways to fill the space between each row. Piled with magazines and newspapers from around the world, the dinette table bristled with so much reading material it's hard to imagine ever reclaiming it for a meal. Geography. History. Politics. Books about the stars and the bottoms of the seas, Taoism, cubism, socialism, Mars. I stood among the stacks of paper, wondering about these lives so dependent on printed matter. Then I recog-nized a familiar sight, a tangible link to the Dan and Nancy I knew: by the doorway lay the canvas bag stuffed with their collapsible kayak.

We left our gear and went out to explore. On the streets, everyone was chattering about the storm. Some of the subways flooded. Offices were closing early. The mid-town tunnel shut down, choked by hemorrhaging sewers.

The wind increased ferociously. Matthew and I scam-pered into a nearby pool hall and shot a few games while we waited for the storm to diminish. From the window, we watched homebound office workers stagger against the gale. By the time we returned to the apartment we were soaking wet, water sloshing in our shoes.

Dan and Nancy had finally gotten back, working long past quitting time. They are social workers, community activists. Nancy works for a neighborhood legal services office in Brooklyn; she's apparently a local heroine there. I could imagine her walking the narrow streets, pausing in the doorway of a Chinese market to speak with an elderly man, her owl-like glasses accenting her compassionate face. Dan works for a big firm in midtown. He is an affable fel-low. He laughs openly, loudly, frequently, his kind face shin-ing through his salt-and-pepper beard, belying his incessant worries about the proximity of robbers.

They had brought home Asian food. We stayed up late, feasting on pad-thai and planning the following day. Then we bulldozed back the books and magazines and unfolded the Hide-a-bed for Matt and me. Outside, the rain still poured, a slanting range of gray lit by ever-burning city lights.

DAYBREAK. THE RAIN SLOWED TO A DRIZZLE. *The New York Times* carried headlines about the storm, with photographs of scuba divers rescuing stranded drivers. Further north, record snowfalls clogged the cities and highways. This was the Great Storm of '92.

Under umbrellas, we walked to the corner for bagels and coffee. Then Nancy took a cab uptown for her class on pre-Columbian art. We would meet her later at Rockefeller Center. Dan took Matt and me for a walk in the neighborhood.

"See that building?" he said, pointing to a brownstone across the street. "Last year the people there tortured their children to death." His usual smile had vanished. His lower lip twitched.

A block further, Dan nodded toward a cross street.

"Guy got torn apart by muggers on that corner," he said. "Didn't have a chance. Over a dozen witnesses, too. Broad daylight. They just walked up to the poor fellow and cut him to ribbons. Lifted his wallet. Walked away."

I felt Matthew hanging closer by my side.

We walked past the pool hall where Matt and I had whiled away the previous afternoon.

"Stay away from this joint," said Dan. "Last month a gang of drug dealers stormed the place, shooting down everyone in sight. Now there are rumors of impending retaliation."

We met Nancy by the ice rink at Rockefeller Center. Even the record rains couldn't dampen the holiday fervor of mid-Manhattan. The drizzly skies made the Christmas lights glisten even more. Taxis and buses flowed like lava through the street, their taillights igniting the air. All around us, the metallic sheen of office buildings banked skyward, their upper floors hidden in mist.

We spent the afternoon zigzagging through the Metropolitan Museum and gawking in Macy's and Bloomingdale's. Dan had wanted to take us to his office in the World Trade Center so we could see the view, but that would have to come on a clearer day. A few months after our visit, while Dan worked at his desk, his building got bombed by terrorists (he had told me he worried it was a potential target).

We stopped for matzo ball soup and pastrami sandwiches at the Carnegie Deli, then went back to Dan and Nancy's. We settled in with tea and baklava.

"You guys have it made, up in Maine," said Dan. "Nice people, no rude manners, no violence. This city is done for. It's only a matter of time before the whole works cave in."

"You could always move," I suggested once more.

"Dan is a dreamer," said Nancy. "I don't think we'll ever leave. We have our families here. Our cultural activities and jobs. Our friends and communities, too. Besides, we're committed to the city: we've got to do our part."

"But, Nancy," he moaned, raising his hands in a gesture of dissent, "someday we'll have no choice. Things can only worsen; Armageddon, the apocalypse, wars between the races! Sooner or later, we'll have to go."

"Maybe," she said. "We'll see."

They were always dreaming about living somewhere else. They had considered Seattle and Portland, Oregon, but bands of skinheads there had frightened them. Even in Stonington, the appearance of a Jewish-Asian couple was an oddity that generated disquieting stares from many of the fishermen. Was there any other place for them? How odd that this couple, their way of life a demonstration of tolerance, might live forever in a city where man's inhumanity to man seemed a constant threat.

IN THE MORNING, WE ROSE EARLY to get a good start on our trip back to Maine. Dan and Nancy joined us for a walk to the corner for bagels to take home to Judi. Rivulets still ran and broad pools of standing water filled the intersections. Here and there, a fire truck waited, a police car, a public works van, their warning lights blinking, while exhausted city workers in day-glow raincoats sat on the bumpers waiting for the water to recede. Overhead, the sun worked to digest the film of gray that lingered.

Matthew drove the car up from the garage and we said our goodbyes. According to the radio, the Major Deegan and the commuter parkways out of the city were still iffy, their low spots inundated with mud and cars left abandoned in the flood. Fortunately, Interstate 95 had gone unscathed; it would be an easy drive home. Following Dan's directions, we crossed Broadway and splashed through puddles all the way to the FDR Drive.

We mounted the skyway and broke above the city, rising to meet the laundered skies. Patches of sunshine emerged. It felt so good! Too good, perhaps—so entranced was I with blue skies and warm sun, I failed to watch the road signs: we missed the turn to I-95! The spur of roadway beneath us fell downward, back to the city's clutches. Behind us, our escape way to Maine vanished, blocked by a DO NOT ENTER sign.

The freeway had dumped us in a desolate place. There were no standing buildings; only rubble covered the empty blocks between the shattered streets. Years ago, decrepit tenements must have been bulldozed away, the target of a now-stalled urban renewal project. On the other side of this godforsaken acreage, deteriorating projects still stood, and behind them in the distance, more prosperous neighborhoods. We waited alone at a traffic light, Matthew and me, our idling Toyota, and the signal that wouldn't turn green.

Suddenly, from somewhere behind us, a disheveled woman in a ragged coat appeared. She walked hurriedly toward us, knowing she had to catch us before the light changed. I felt a twinge of fear. Is she armed? Is she a decoy, the accomplice of a gang of muggers waiting to spring from the sewers? Should I stomp on the accelerator and speed away? Too late! Panting, she leaned toward my window, which, on this fresh and sunny morning, I had left half-lowered. She stooped close and stared into my face. Her hair hung damp and stringy, and her coat smelled musty, as if she had just emerged from some mildewed hiding place. Everything about her seemed soiled: her face, her hands, her hair, so dirty that even "the storm of the century" had failed to rinse her clean. In her bony hand, she clutched a Styrofoam cup, its rim crumbled and grimy. She raised it to my window.

"Help me," she gasped. The words clattered from her mouth like a death rattle.

In spite of her rags and her unnerving presence, there seemed a familiarity about her. The haunted look and the sunken eyes, the carved lines across the brow—they were universal features branded into my consciousness from years of evening news and pages of *Time*: the mother in Sarajevo, the tribeswoman from Bangladesh, the Somali mother with the dead child in her arms. But I was not in Bangladesh—this was New York City. Only blocks away, other American women swished through the aisles of Bloomingdale's, wrapped in mink and ermine, buying exotic Christmas presents, while their chauffeurs waited in limousines.

I tried to dig in my pocket, but my bucket seat was too confining and my seat belt held me down. The light turned green. A nudge against my arm: Matthew poked me with a crumpled dollar. I took it and dropped it in her cup. She scurried away without a word of thanks. That meager bill would soon be spent on a bowl of soup, a swig of wine, a needle, or a pill, whatever she used to ease her pain.

Who was this wispy, homeless woman? Maybe prior to landing in the street, she had been raised in some squeaky-clean suburb of Connecticut. Or she could be a factory worker driven from the Newark slums by an abusive husband, or an Upper East Side dowager robbed of her livelihood by cheating bankers. She could be almost anyone. Then I realized: this wizened tramp could even be my toilet-riding Godiva from thirty years before.

I looked for her in the rearview mirror, but I saw only crazed pavement, muddy earth, and the backdrop of hunkered tenements that surrounded us like an ancient coliseum. Vanished. She had merged back into the weedy lots and alleys where so many others languish, but her image would not leave my mind.

Finally, Matthew found the on-ramp: Interstate 95. We curled again to the heavens and left New York behind. As we drove north, the pools of water became piles of snow. I drove mechanically, feeling little Christmas cheer. There are too many poor people in the world, too much war, too many government billions wasted on weapons and subterfuge.

As we drove across the Piscataqua bridge back to Maine, I thought again of the beggar woman. How many more are there like her? Someday, when there is no more government safety net, no collective will to offer a hand, no jobs, no chances, no choices, no hope, maybe the wretched homeless like her, the immigrants, the jobless and broke, the addicts and hookers and sick will all swarm by the millions from the subways and parks, grabbing hold of any handy bludgeon or shard of pointy glass . . . and attack.

Meanwhile, here *I* am on Isle au Haut!

Sometimes I feel guilty, leaving others to wrestle with the nation's problems. But long ago, when we first came to this gentle island, we made the choice to leave behind those urban stresses and build a sanctuary where folks like Dan and Nancy could come for relaxation.

They make choices too—although, like most New Yorkers, I doubt they'll ever leave. During blackouts, tidal

waves, and urban riots, I can imagine them hanging on, trying to make things better.

But every August their hearts and minds will gravitate
northeastward, with that habitual need to flee the city for
their annual summer vacation. If the airlines are on strike,
it won't matter. If the highways are closed by uncollected
garbage, civil strife, and the rubble of hurricanes or earth-
quakes, that's no problem either. With the irrepressible
instinct of lemmings plunging toward the sea, they'll snap
together their kayak and launch it into the East River. Even
if the buildings crumble around them, even if the bridges
twist and tumble, no matter how disastrous the times, Dan
and Nancy will escape Manhattan, if only for a little while.

I can envision them now: at first only an elongated
speck on the evening horizon, behind them a crimson sunset over distant troubled cities. But as they creep across the
bay, I'll eventually recognize the familiar shape of their
approaching kayak and their silhouettes with synchronized
paddles wheeling. Closer and closer they'll come. There's
Nancy's broad smile! Dan's salt-and-pepper beard! And
when the battle-scarred bow of their kayak limps through
the waves to our float, I'll be down at the pier to greet
them. They'll present me with a dozen fresh bagels (poppy
seed and onion), then settle in to enjoy the scented woods,
the untouched shore, to savor the delights from Judi's oven
and sleep soundly through the nights. Then, at the end of
their holiday, they'll shove off refreshed in their kayak and
paddle back to the city to continue on with the fight.

REALLY GOOD BAGELS

5 cups unsifted flour
3 Tbs. sugar
3/4 Tbs. salt
2 packages yeast or 2 Tbs. yeast
2 Tbs. margarine
1 Tbs. sugar
2 tsp. salt
1 egg white mixed with 1 Tbs. water

Mix 1 1/2 cups flour with the sugar, salt, and yeast. Heat 1 1/2 cups water and margarine to 120 degrees. Add to dry ingredients. Beat two minutes. Add 1/2 cup flour. Beat two minutes. Stir in enough flour to make a stiff dough. Knead 10 minutes. Let rise in a greased bowl for 1 hour.

Punch dough down. Divide into 12 pieces. In large skillet simmer 1 inch water. Add salt and sugar. Roll each piece of dough into a bagel shape and place in simmering water. Cook 3 minutes on one side, 2 minutes on the other. Turn again for 2 minutes. Drain on towels.

Roll in poppy seeds, sesame seeds, or a cooked mixture of butter and onions. Place on greased baking sheet. Brush with egg mixture. Bake at 375 degrees for 20–25 minutes, turning once. Always sweet and chewy, so make sure you allow more than one per diner.

18
MORE ABOUT CHLORESSA

July 30, 1993

FROM ATOP THE LIGHTHOUSE I WATCHED THE FOG. For days it hadn't lifted, persistent fog, ever-present, starving us for sun. Below me lapped a sea so gauzed in mist I could barely see it. My familiar woods were hidden in the grayness. Distant foghorns moaned. Cloaked and hidden, all my domain seemed safely wrapped in woolly blankets, but I worried about Chloressa.

She's such a fickle machine. I'm always lecturing the kitchen crew:

Lighten up on the detergent, please,
or Chloressa will froth and foam.
A deluge of suds will overflow her hatches
and drive us from our home.
And don't overdose on the Clorox, either,
the consequences are dire:
You'll annihilate my microbe armies
who chew apart the mire.

But most of all, I anguished over the
inevitable day when an official from the
Department of Environmental Protection

would appear at our door for the annual inspection. Judi tells me not to worry—but Chloressa is my responsibility, the center of my attention, the standard which measures my skill, my knowledge, my worth. Judi doesn't understand: I would be the wounded one if Chloressa fails to pass muster. As I gazed into the fog, below me a young woman suddenly emerged from the vapors, light-footed as a doe. She wore jeans and boots and a loose-fitting shirt, appropriately dressed for island work. She carried a blue plastic case, which she placed on the ground near the house. She was obviously an official of some sort, sent to make sure we were following the rules. I instantly became distressed. Were the thermometers in the refrigerators? Was the cellar storeroom clean? Had Heather scrubbed the johns?

The woman gazed at the shore, unaware of me hovering above her. The fog swirled around her, an aura that left her half real and half apparition, a mermaid in the mist.

"Hello," I called through the smoke. "Can I be of any help?"

"Yes," she hollered back, looking for me in the clouds. "I'm here from the Department of Environmental Protection."

"Cripes!" I muttered, worried about all the imperfections of my sewage treatment plant; the blackish waters exposing a lack of treatment time, the odors too rich to pass the test of a discriminating nose, the tell-tale crust of hardened crud that caked the overflow valve—there were a dozen more defects that should have been tended. But now, I could only pray.

Down the spiral stairs I scurried, emerging from the tower. She waited by the front porch while I walked toward her through the vapors, rubbing my palms against my pants to remove the cold sweat in case she extended a hand. Outwardly, I was debonair and charming, my most perfect hotelier self.

As I took the last few steps, the fog no longer obscured her. Pretty woman, rugged in a feminine way. Her hazel eyes sparkled; I sensed a smoldering inside. "I'm here to inspect your state-licensed secondary sewage treatment system," she said sweetly. "Please show me where it is."

There was a wholesome friendliness that, with her natural beauty, made my senses twitter. She enchanted me. While I babbled foolishly about my sewage plant, she trailed behind me to the edge of the woods. There, I parted the spruce boughs that gleamed with foggy moisture, exposing my hidden path to Chloressa.

The day before I had hosed down the system and added chlorine tablets to the contact tank. Now, veiled in a shroud of fog and surrounded by attendant spruce, Chloressa reigned with queenly splendor. The young lady with the plastic case listened attentively while I explained my procedures: the finicky switches for starting the generator, the twenty-four-hour clock, the manual rotations of the dial, the stirring and coaxing, the evening visits, the hours of waiting in the woods. I showed her the neatly coiled hose I use to bathe Chloressa, the rakes and brushes to clean her screens. We climbed over fallen trees and through patches of raspberry bushes to inspect the chlorine contact tank. Then we clambered down the shore and followed the serpentine discharge line that flushes away the gray water, injecting it below the tide. There, hungry creatures from the deep wait for a remnant of Judi's delicacies, a half-digested flake of sanitized chicken breast or the enzyme-riddled residue of scallops, herbs, and butter.

The young lady watched with rapt attention while I spoke, occasionally asking a question about the quality of our toilet paper or about my schedule for running the machine. Beside us purred Chloressa.

The more I explained Chloressa's care, the more the young woman focused on me: it felt so wonderful, so flirtatious, so free—the excitement of an old married man capturing a pretty girl's attention.

She complimented me on the care I give Chloressa, while complaining of other men on other islands who neglect their sewage plants, men who fail to cultivate their bacteria count, who rush too fast and don't use enough aeration time, who assault the sea with batches of mushy paper, slimy Pampers, and untreated poop.

"You're creative and thorough and thoughtful," she said, "in the way you treat your sewage." My feet shuffled nervously in the pine needles.

"Thanks," I said, blushing.

Her hazel eyes conveyed the softness of the forest around us. The touch of the fog moved against us, nudging us softly, pushing us closer, while Chloressa pulsed in heartbeat time, her voice a reminder of gentle pleasures; the soothing vibrations of her pulsing pumps, her gushing sounds, the warmth of her smooth plastic skin. The young woman shared these sensations with me; I saw it in the way she watched me, in the tone of her voice, in the way we lingered there, wondering if there were other questions, other matters still undone.

Soon the mailboat would come. Husbands and wives waited in other lives. There was work to be done. Patterns were already set, the world turning in age-old orbit. The exchange of a smile, a twinkling eye—these were our universe, our moment in time.

The young woman pulled a clipboard from the plastic case and scribbled notes on a triplicate form, dashing off a column of "S's" (satisfactory) down the lefthand margin:

[S] Aeration

[S] Odors

[S] Scum

[S] Pump stations

[S] Disinfection

[S] Effluent quality

[S] Maintenance

COMMENTS: Cared for very well by owner.

Then she signed her name across the bottom and tore off the pink copy for me. I took it from her, feeling a spark as the bit of paper passed between us.

"Please let me know if you need me," she said. "I'll send you literature on biodegradable single-ply and chemicals to shrink your sludge . . . just let me know . . . I'll do what I can . . . I know you treat your system right."

She took a step into the fog. Hesitated. Took one step more. Turned for another look. Her pace quickened then, and as the curtains of fog closed around her, she turned one last time to speak, before she disappeared.

"Call on me if I can help . . ." Her words trailed away in mist.

I watched her leave, wondering where she lived, what her life was like. The young woman with the blue plastic case had left me with only a scrap of paper, my sewage treatment report. I scanned the page once more. "S" for everything. I took a final look, reading every line—and then I saw the little space where she had signed her name:

INSPECTED BY: *Clarissa*

SCALLOPS SAUTÉED IN
HERBS AND BUTTER

1 1/2 pounds fresh scallops
1/4 cup butter
1 Tbs. chopped parsley
1 tsp. fresh lemon juice
1 cup bread crumbs
3 Tbs. parmesan cheese
1/2 clove minced garlic
1 tsp. chopped chives
1/2 cup dry white wine
salt and pepper

Melt butter in small saucepan. Add parsley and lemon juice. In separate
bowl, mix crumbs, cheese, garlic, and chives. Place scallops in a buttered
casserole dish. Pour wine and lemon butter mixture over them. Sprinkle
with seasoned bread crumbs, salt, and pepper. Bake 15 minutes at 400
degrees. Makes generous portions for 6. Serve with rice and veggies.

19

THE NIGHT WE OVERBOOKED

August 18, 1993

ECONOMY OF SCALE; SIZE IS WHAT COUNTS. Try to earn a buck by renting a single bike or sautéing shrimp for only two. Where would this country be without the think-biggers, the Rockefellers, Mellons, Du Ponts, and their ilk? Applying the principle of supply and demand came easy for me: we mushroomed in size, from three rooms to four and then to five. Next, I converted the woodshed into our own little dream house, with a snug bedroom upstairs. But I wanted the inn to keep on growing, so I set up a futon for ourselves in our downstairs living area and started renting our bedroom. That made six rental rooms. Filled all the time. Money, money, money, the dollars rolled in. We paid our bills, stashed extra bucks in our IRAs, and still had change left over to splurge at the Mex on chicken fajitas with rice and beans. I thought my empire could expand forever, just by adding rooms.

Judi felt differently.

"You're not the one who cleans the bathrooms," she said. "You don't plan the menu, either. Try cutting twelve pieces from an apple pie, or dividing a baking dish of seafood crepes among a dozen people."

173

But I stared out to sea, with visions of converting the boathouse into yet another rental room, although I would have to displace Matthew, who slept there in the rafters during summer vacation. It's irresistible, the way the boathouse hangs over the water, the surf washing underneath, secluded and rustic. Guests would kill for the chance to sleep there, to gaze at the sunset and make whoopee in the loft.

"No!" said Judi. "Try waiting tables some night. I'd like to see you squeeze between all those chairs. And the noise! Imagine what another couple would add."

In spite of Judi's opposition, I couldn't help fantasizing. Each time I met the mailboat, I'd count the couples climbing the ramp. Two by two, they flocked ashore, like pilgrims arriving on promised land. Two, four, six, eight, I counted with dreams of growing numbers. Ten, twelve, they kept coming—I'd like to see a dozen more.

I had to admit, though, more rooms would pose a few technical problems. For example, Chloressa can handle only so much sewage, and our anemic well sometimes goes dry in the middle of summer droughts. But with the additional income generated, we could build a water tower, bring in sewers and power lines—if only there were a city to supply them. How about a string of little cabins, each with a deck and picture window? Maybe a sauna, a new dining room, a shuffleboard court and a swimming pool. We could do most anything: that's the advantage of economy of scale.

I felt like a tycoon with my six rental rooms. *Jeffrey Burke Enterprises,* now that sounds cool! Lighthouses were only a beginning. Think of the obsolete trains, the covered bridges, the flotillas of mothballed battleships, all waiting for *Jeffrey Burke Enterprises* to convert them into inns of warmth and distinction. I'd be an icon in the innkeeping world, the object of admiration and envy. With all my wealth and

fame, I'd need a mistress, too (isn't that the way it's done?).
Maybe the enchanting inspector from the Department of
Environmental Protection, or the exotic beauty who
declined Paul's wedding proposal, maybe even a movie star,
or an award-winning poet, or a Jazzercise workout lady.
Who knows what willing candidate might arrive on the
5:20 mailboat!

Late this summer Maggie and I waited in the
boathouse for the afternoon arrival of *Mink*. It had been a
tough day. Lisa had opened her own bakery over at the old
schoolhouse on the east side, so we had hired a new chef,
Patience, an intern from the New England Culinary
Institute. We were weary and the new cook was in a foul
mood. Already, her hollandaise had curdled and she had
scorched the bottom of her lemon tea cake. Angrily she
thrashed about the kitchen, her wide girth sending tidal
waves of ill will surging through the inn. When the mailboat pulled in, I trudged down the ramp to receive the new
arrivals, hoping there would be no requests for low-sodium
diets, no folks with food allergies, no other problems to further antagonize the misnamed Patience.

Two, four, six, the new arrivals clambered off the boat.
Eight, ten, twelve, with bags and bikes and rolled-up kites.
Fourteen, sixteen . . . what? No, it couldn't be! Fourteen?
Sixteen? I must have miscounted, what with all the luggage
and people and gear.

I rushed toward the house, Maggie bounding along
beside me, trying to crowd past the file of new guests that
meandered through the woods.

"Wait," I yelled. "There are too many of you. Something's wrong. There's been a mistake."

A sense of panic rippled through the crowd. While trying to maintain their self-control and a modicum of dignity,
the more nimble guests vaulted up the front steps, dashed

through the door, and raced to the registration desk, leaving their duffel bags strewn across the porch to slow down the opposition. The consequences were obvious for those without a room: this was Isle au Haut, rugged and wild. The distant village offers no warm lodgings, no bus depot or rental cars.

Judi stood in the living room welcoming folks, the way she always does. In her hand was the guest list. Two, four, six, eight, they crowded in, filling the hallway and the dining room. Ten, twelve, fourteen, sixteen . . . Judi's mouth gaped open. She tried to reconcile the surging numbers with the trembling list she held. "Please bear with us a moment," she stammered. "We seem to have a problem."

I raced around to the back of the house, hoping to see Buster coming up the path to retrieve four people who were supposed to have gotten off somewhere else. But *Mink* was on her way, plunging hard for Stonington.

Regaining her composure the best she could, Judi went to her task with a nervous smile. "Let's see, now. Tom and Margie Blivens?"

"That's us," said a couple in the corner.

"You're in the Keeper's Room," said Judi. "The pink room right up the stairs. Now, Berta and Stan?"

"Right here," cried two more, eager to claim their room.

"Horizon Room. On your right at the top of the stairs," directed Judi.

Judi focused on the list. Which room should she call next? Beginning to feel she was playing Russian roulette, she clicked off two more, knowing that all too soon the six chambers would be accounted for.

"In the Sunrise Room we have Richard and Bella Carlson. Their friends, the Drearys, are in the Woodshed. Jeffrey will show you the way." Four more relieved faces.

"Next, Sharon Lyons and Donald Plows," Judi called. "You're in the Garret, all the way up to the third floor." A couple hovering in the hallway lifted their luggage and started up the stairs.

"Wait a minute," snorted a tall man behind Judi. "The Garret is our room. I have my confirmation right here to prove it."

He looked like a lawyer. Said his name was Sneed. His wife, a woman with dangling lighthouse earrings and a gaudy silk bandanna, crowded in beside him as if she were prepared to open her leather satchel and start filing legal suits. Their cronies, the Baldwins, were right there at his elbow. They had confirmations, too, claiming the Oil House was theirs for the night (our list had Bernie and Rachel Valdez written clearly in black and white). The haughty lawyer-man and his arrogant sidekicks got pretty nasty, insisting their reservations were guaranteed. Sharon and Donald and the Valdez couple waited politely.

The confirmations were in our handwriting. All four couples had valid reservations for the last two rooms. Somehow, we had overbooked.

Because of the lawyer's hostile attitude, Judi hustled Sharon and Donald and the Valdezes into the last two rooms. (As a union shop steward for many years, Judi learned never to cower to bullying attorneys.) So the Sneed mob waited, bitter and threatening. There was nowhere for them to stay, nowhere else to go. They kept muttering, "Well, there *must* be somewhere to sleep," while staring covetously out the window toward the woodshed, toward my inner sanctum where my futon hides.

Judi thought of a solution. Matthew was taking care of Mitzi Archibald's cats at the next house down the shore, while Mitzi was off-island for the week. Matt agreed to sleep at Mitzi's for the night and relinquish his loft in the

boathouse. Fortunately, the lawyer and his buddy thought it
would be fun sleeping over the water and eagerly rushed to
inspect it.

"Far out!" they exclaimed, climbing into the loft.

But their wives didn't like Judi's plan for the two of
them to sleep on the living room sofa. They kept eyeing my
woodshed.

"You're welcome to have our room," Judi finally con-
ceded, ignoring the jabs from my elbow. "Jeffrey will show
you the way, as soon as he changes the sheets and tidies up
the room."

Patience was furious. Extra seatings at the dining table
would be a defilement of her minutely calculated servings
of eggplant Parmesan soup and her dozen chilled wine
glasses filled with *crème du chocolat*, and there were only
enough poached salmon steaks for twelve. Fuming, she bay-
oneted a cabbage with her boning knife and kicked over a
kitchen chair, then stormed to the fridge to sacrifice the
chicken breast intended for the next day's picnic lunches.
Heather rushed to the garden to pick more greens, while
Judi and I searched for additional chairs. Wrestling an extra
table into the dining room, I smashed my knuckles against
the door jamb.

There were lines outside the bathrooms, lines at the
guest register, lines going out to look at the surf. Patience
complained and swore while she and Judi threw together
extra dressing, baked another torte, peeled potatoes, and
diced more onions. The cookstoves raged. Steam billowed
from the pantry where poor Matthew labored over the
sink, scrubbing load after load, as if Patience were out to
punish the world by dirtying every pot. But at least things
were under control, the problems all solved.

Except for one: where was *I* going to sleep? Mitzi's
house was out of the question (I'm allergic to cats). Albert

and Lori had company. Ed's boat was crammed with too much junk. I could sleep outside, but it looked like rain. Then Judi remembered Mitzi's empty bunkhouse: it was deep in the woods by the swamp.

Late that night, after our sixteen guests had been fed and entertained, after Patience and Heather and Matt finally got done in the kitchen, after the last guest had showered, after the last flush of the john, after the last squeaky bedroom door had closed, we blew out the lanterns and shut down the gaslights and finally got out of the inn. Exhausted, we trailed down the hill towards Mitzi's. Maggie ran ahead, crashing in and out of the woods, somehow under the illusion that we were having fun.

Stumbling into the dark bunkhouse, we found it cold, damp, gloomy, about as hospitable as a morgue. We searched for a match to light the gaslights, but couldn't find any. In the dying glow of our flashlight, we groped about, banged our shins, climbed into bed.

Judi got the top bunk. She felt it would be better there, where Maggie wouldn't bother her. I climbed in underneath. My feet were killing me and my knuckles still ached from the slamming they took moving the table. Around my throbbing head buzzed a squadron of bloodthirsty mosquitoes, but I was so tired I didn't even care. I only wanted to sleep.

Maggie paced. Unfamiliar territory. Too many exciting smells from the swamp. Too many unknown sounds. Outside, a crash in the woods. She howled and charged the door, barking to get out, her Great Dane hunting instincts ignited. A scraping sound on the roof . . . she whined and growled. She trotted from door to window, sniffing the air, staring into the blackness. Her toenails clicked on the bare wood floor . . . the planks squeaked from her weight. I would never get to sleep.

I only had one choice.

"Come 'ere, Mag," I called. "Come sleep with Daddy."

I scootched against the wall; she was beside me with a single bound. She nuzzled me and stretched out, her rear legs protruding over the end of the bed. She yawned and licked and snuggled closer, laying her head on my arm. There I was, exhausted and sore, intimidated by a moody cook, driven out of my bed by big-city lawyers, starving and cold, slapping at mosquitoes in a log cabin in the swamp, sleeping with the family dog. Something wasn't right. I lay awake and evaluated *Jeffrey Burke Enterprises.*

Maybe six rooms were enough. In fact, maybe six rooms were too many. Five would be better. Ten people are better than twelve. You can get ten nice pieces out of an apple pie. And there's far less noise in the dining room, and Chloressa could do a better job.

I didn't need a mistress, either. I stared through the blackness above me where Judi lay suspended in sleep. Over the sounds of the swamp, the wind in the trees, the creak of the roof, the breath of Maggie in my ear, I could sense the beat of Judi's heart, synchronized with mine. I remembered thirty-two years ago. We were eighteen. We had run away to New Orleans. My smoking Chevy broke down in Jackson Square. We sold it to a transvestite named Freddy for fifty dollars—he never sent the check. We found a cheap hotel off Bourbon Street, the Anchor Inn, "World headquarters for the International Women's Wrestling Association." All night we stayed up listening to the dirty blues and hot Dixieland that filled the streets below. In the morning, we walked silently down the long corridor to the bathroom at the end of the hall. It was dark . . . damp . . . windowless. We stood in the concrete shower and unveiled each other. With the little Ivory soaps and the trickle of lukewarm water, we explored and discovered, mapping a course that would stretch forever.

"Judith," I murmured.

No response.

"I've got a great idea," I said. I think we should get smaller. Let's roll back the clock."

"Leave me alone," she mumbled. "I'm tired. I want to go to sleep."

"We'll reclaim our bedroom, the entire woodshed. We could use the space. Matthew will finally be away at college, too. After all these years, wouldn't it be nice to finally have our own little house?"

I heard her turn above me.

"What about 'economy of scale'?" she sighed, drooping a leg over the side of her bunk.

I pushed Maggie off the bed and flipped back the sheet.

"Economy of scale?" I said. "Let's leave that to Howard Johnson's."

EGGPLANT PARMESAN SOUP

1 eggplant, peeled, diced, soaked in salt water for 30 minutes
4 Tbs. olive oil
3 medium yellow onions, chopped
10 medium cloves garlic, crushed
2 Tbs. basil, diced
1 Tbs. crushed red pepper
1 Tbs. oregano
salt and pepper to taste
2 15-oz. cans organic whole peeled tomatoes, chopped with juice
3 cups water
1 1/4 cups organic tomato puree
2 Tbs. soy sauce
1/4 cup white wine
Parmesan cheese
Italian or French bread

Sauté garlic and onion in olive oil until tender. Add red pepper and sauté 2 minutes. Add remaining spices and sauté 1 minute. Add eggplant and sauté until tender. Add remaining ingredients, bring to boil, and simmer for 30 minutes or longer. Adjust seasonings. TO SERVE: Place a piece of crusty Italian or French bread in each bowl. Pour soup over bread and top with freshly grated Parmesan cheese. Garnish with a dusting of Hungarian paprika. Makes 14 to 16 decent portions, but only 10 would be much nicer.

Note: I tried repeatedly to get Patience's recipe for this soup, but she is an elusive wandering chef who is hard to trace and never returns my calls; from across the country, I receive only vague rumors about her kitchen tantrums and frequent notices from the Department of Unemployment Compensation increasing my contribution rate. Fortunately, our current chef, delightful Elke Christofferson, artfully recreated this gastronomical delight.

ISLE AU HAUT

FERRY

Nathan I.

Mouse I.

Birch Pt

Laundry Cove

Flake I.

Private Dock

Northwest Cove

Rosebud Island

Elephant Head

Town Landing

Pt.

Store

Kimball Head

Kimball Island 188

120

ISL V.

P.O.

Marsh Cove Head

Acadia Park Ranger Station

Marsh Cove

Thorofare

BLACK DINA

Isle au Haut

Robinson Pt.

The Keeper's House (Inn)

HARBOR TRAIL

ISLE AU HAUT BAY

BALD MTN.

BOWDITCH

ACADI

(SEASONAL)

BOWDITCH MTN.

FERRY

Trial Pt.

DUCK

The Seal Trap

Moore Harbor

Eli Creek

LONG

PASS

Moore Head

Deep Cove

WENTWORTH MTN. 201

NAT

Shark Pt.

DUCK HARBOR

NAT

Merchant B

Ebens Head

EBENS

RIDGE

Duck Harbor

PARK

Duck Harbor